LIGHT
IN YOUR
DARKNESS

by
Harry Greenwood

TORBAY PUBLISHING

Distributed in the U.S.A. by

Torbay Publishing
1652 E. Del Rio Drive
Tempe, AZ 85282
Phone (602) 838-2142

Preface

IN the last few years I have travelled extensively both in home countries and abroad and I have been overwhelmed by the great need of God's children. Because of my love for the Body of Christ, I have sought to find an answer to this need - a need which I believe God has already met according to His word. If they knew the truth, the truth would make them free.[1]

It is God's purpose that all His children should be one hundred per cent free from need, whether it be in their spiritual, physical or material life and it is this conviction that has compelled me to write this book. I have been conscious of the inspiration of the Holy Spirit throughout and would therefore ask the reader to discern spiritually what has been written, rather than to analyse it naturally.[2]

It is imperative that a child of God should have a revelation (the revealed truth of the word by the Spirit) -

> for his spiritual life
> > for his physical life
> > > and for his material life.

Having this revelation, he can then live by FAITH in what God says and not by what Satan dictates through adverse circumstances. I believe that God, through this book, will set His saints free from being continually in need, thereby advertising in their lives the provision of God. Being free then, they can minister to those who are not yet in this revelation.

The Spirit of God is leading us into what we are in Christ,

---

[1] JOHN 8:32   [2] 1 COR. 2:14,15

what we have in Christ and what we can do through Christ. We must remember that we have a new covenant which is legal in heaven and on earth, so that we can be confident in God's provision.

I have not sold my 'Epistles' in the past, but God has shown me that I should sell this book in the countries which can afford to buy it. The money received can then be used to give the book to countries which cannot afford to buy it, such as Africa, Central and South America, India etc. The profit from every book that is sold will be used to provide another copy free in one of those countries.

My prayer is that the Holy Spirit will bring you into the fullness of all that Christ has accomplished for you through the cross.

"Beloved, I wish above all things that thou mayest prosper and be in health, even as thy soul prospereth."[3]

---

[3] 3 JOHN 2

Foreword

In Him was life, and the life was the light of men, and the light shines on in the darkness, for the darkness has never overpowered it ....(John 1 v 4/5 Amp). The truth, which makes you free .... from darkness bondage and condemnation - If there is a need for today, it is that the truth should be expressed in the lives of Christians. This book, written, I believe, under the anointing of the Holy Spirit, helps us to understand some of the simple truths of scripture; and these truths are so brought together and confirmed by reference to the Word of God, that it brings fresh light and challenge to us every day of our lives. Each chapter, from faith, healing to health, God's prosperity, Life in the Spirit, becomes a challenge from God afresh, but it also, as the light of truth dawns on us, brings the revelations that it is possible for each of us to experience what God says daily.

I have known the author intimately now for many years, since a few weeks after his conversion, and have seen the challenge of all he says in this book taking place in his own life, and have seen the evidence of what God says become true in his experience. I see not only him, but also his wife and family walk by faith. I see them live in health. Everything that surrounds this family, shows that they live in prosperity to the glory of God, in whom they have trusted.

I have seen Harry minister and live in the power of the Holy Spirit for many years now, and pray that this book may be a challenge and inspiration to you, so that on further reference to God's Word, you will realise that the light continues to shine in the darkness, but will only be seen to do so, when you realise by faith, that the light is within you and can and will break out when you take God at His word and believe. Then the light which is in you will shine out through you to others and bring light in their darkness.

For today
>   God is preparing a whole body
>   living in the Spirit
>   to bring to birth a full revelation
>   and manifestation of Christ.

John Hutchison.   Paignton.

Contents

CHAPTER ONE

Faith

THE JUST SHALL LIVE BY FAITH

Heb. 2:4   Rom. 1:17   Gal. 3:11   Heb. 10:38

"WITHOUT faith it is impossible to please God"[1] for "whatsoever is not of faith is sin."[2]

If we walked by faith and not by sight, we should not be so easily defeated and overcome by the things that come against us, for "this is the victory that overcometh the world, even our faith."[3]

We believe that
THE LIFE OF CHRIST IN US *HAS* OVERCOME THE DEVIL
but this is not sufficient in itself, because
THE FAITH THAT IS IN US *MUST* OVERCOME THE WORLD

We accept that the world is outside us, because we believe we are not of the world, but quite often the world is in us, in our thinking. Paul said, "be not conformed to this world" - that is, to their thinking and to their values - but "be ye transformed by the renewing of your mind."[4]

The Israelites had lived in Egypt for forty years as slaves and then they were set free. Their whole thinking had to be changed to visualise the provision of God to enable them to live in the

---

[1] HEB. 11:6   [2] ROM. 14:23   [3] 1 JOHN 5:4   [4] ROM. 12:2

1

promised land. It did not take God long to bring the children of Israel out of Egypt, but it took Him forty years to get Egypt out of them. By this we can see the importance of the mind, for "as a man thinketh in his heart, so is he."[5]

Just as God's chosen people today have been separated from the world by a new birth and given an incorruptible inheritance, we must now possess that inheritance as sons, for slaves have no inheritance.

We normally act on information received by our minds, but our believing will determine whether we are sons or slaves and whether we are free or imprisoned. Since we act on information from our minds, and react according to that information, the world is no longer outside, but it is inside our minds challenging us.

For example,
    the world says we are in need
    but God says we are in His supply.

We are continually surrounded with evidence received through our senses which brings our minds into subjection to the natural realm. The only evidence we have in the spiritual realm is what God says out of *HIS* knowledge to deliver us from what we know through our natural senses.

To give you a practical example: when I arrived in Los Angeles I discovered that I had missed my connecting flight to New Zealand and was informed by the lady behind the ticket counter that there were no more seats on any plane leaving for New Zealand for the next two days. I knew that God was sending me to New Zealand and the information I received from the world was preventing me from carrying out what God had told me to do. I knew there was another source of information available to me, so I went to my Heavenly Father, reached out to the Heavenly Booking Office by faith and received a seat on the next plane leaving for New Zealand. The only way to overcome the information the world had given me was to receive information from heaven.

I received my seat by faith, went back to the booking counter and asked for a seat on the next plane leaving for New Zealand. The lady looked at me strangely and went through the usual routine on the computer. She was quite amazed and said, "There has been a cancellation and there is a seat available on the next flight to New Zealand." This I could have told her, for I did not come for a seat, I came *with* a seat. The information I received from the world was *overcome by my faith* in what God had said.

No matter how technical and sophisticated man and his equipment may become, my Lord has the last word on my itinerary, because He had the first word, "Go ye into all the world."[6]

FAITH OVERCOMES THE WORLD -
not some of it,
but *all of it.*

We now know that FAITH is the KEY to living and walking in the Spirit, for -
God can only speak to our faith, and the
Word of God can only be acted upon
by faith.

So God moves through our faith to fulfil His purposes.

"Now faith is the assurance (the confirmation, the title-deed) of the things (we) hope for, being the proof of things (we) do not see and the conviction of their reality - faith perceiving as real fact what is not revealed to the senses."[7]

FAITH
sees the invisible,
believes the incredible
and does the impossible.

---

[6] MARK 16:15   [7] HEB. 11:1 (AMP)

The foundation for our faith is what Christ has accomplished for us on the cross - a salvation that delivers the whole man from the power of the devil *AND* keeps him free as he walks in the Spirit by faith.

We have emphasized what Christ accomplished on the cross and that He brought to an end everything that the devil had started. Then why are we frightened to say what Christ began?

He brought the end of sin
     and the beginning of *righteousness*
He brought the end of sickness
     and the beginning of *health*
He brought the end of poverty
     and the beginning of *prosperity*
He brought the end of death
     and the beginning of *eternal life*

We should therefore be living - not at the cross, but beyond the cross, in the finished work of Christ.

What Christ gave up at Calvary

    His life
       His health
       His righteousness
       His wealth

He wants back in His Body - the Church.

We now see how important it is to live by faith in God's Word.

Most Christians believe that they do not have enough faith, but let us consider what the Bible says.

God has dealt to us the measure of faith[8]
    — this represents quantity.
Paul said he lived by the faith of the Son of God[9]
    — this represents quality.

---

[8] ROM. 12:3   [9] GAL. 2:20

4

The quality and quantity of our faith should not be questioned because Jesus Christ is the author and finisher of our faith.[10]

It is not that we do not have enough faith - that would be denying God's word - yet when we look around, we see others who seem to have more faith than we have. They may have more *in operation* but the fact remains that we have the same quantity and quality of faith. The only difference is that we do not all have the same amount of doubt, fear and unbelief preventing faith from being used.

It is not *more* faith we need,
but
less doubt, fear and unbelief,

for these prevent faith coming into operation. God gave us faith when we came to Christ - "By grace are ye saved through faith; and that not of yourselves: it is the gift of God."[11]

Then how do we rid ourselves of doubt, fear and unbelief? Simply by waiting on the Lord, for in His presence all these things die. Many people have felt that after fasting and praying they have a new faith, but this is not so - they have rid themselves of the fear, doubt and unbelief which prevented their faith from working perfectly.

While not denying the existence of the negative, FAITH LOOKS TO THE POSITIVE and gives it substance and evidence.

"Having nothing, and yet possessing all things."[12] Faith allows us to call the things which are not, as though they were.

Now we must distinguish between our faith to receive and experience His life - and faith to minister that life. Because God has given us the faith of the Son of God to live and experience His life, out of our commitment to Him we come into the faith to minister that life. Faith for ministry is different from faith for

---

[10] HEB. 12:2   [11] EPH. 2:8   [12] 2 COR. 6:10

life.

Faith for life deals with what we need.

Faith for ministry deals with what other people need.

We can be assured of this one fact, that we have enough faith to fulfil our ministry, for God has dealt the measure of faith to every person for his own ministry.[13] Going forward in our relationship with the Lord will deepen and accelerate our ministry.

Many Christians doubt their believing and believe their doubts. They have more faith in the belief that they do not have enough faith than in *the fact* that they do.

If you must doubt . . . .

then doubt your doubting

and BELIEVE YOUR BELIEVING.

Unbelief is the darkroom where we develope our negatives. Instead of being dominated by the negative, FAITH allows us to live in the positive.

The Holy Spirit shows us in God's Word what He has supplied, and faith reaches out its hand and takes it.

The centurion is a typical example of faith.[14] He came for healing for his servant, but he did not bring a body, which meant that there was no way he could receive healing for his servant except through faith. If we come by faith, then the word of God becomes the evidence and it is the only evidence that faith needs. The centurion reached out and said, "Speak the word only" and the word he received in his faith became the evidence of healing for his servant.

THE WORD BECOMES THE EVIDENCE TO FAITH.

The Lord was committed to producing in the servant the evidence the centurion had received in his faith. He did not go home for the evidence - he went home with the evidence.

This is a lesson for all Christians who need healing. We do

---

[13] ROM. 12:3   [14] MATT. 8:5

6

not receive healing first in our physical bodies, but in ⟨...⟩
God is committed to producing in our bodies the re⟨...⟩
have already received in our faith.

The new creation only works through our believing what
God says.

> "We have received, not the spirit of the world,
>   but the Spirit which is of God;
>   that we might KNOW the things
>   that are freely given to us
>   of God."[15]

Shall he not with him also freely give us all things?"[16]

We live by faith in what God says we ARE and HAVE in
Christ Jesus; we are complete in Him.[17]

> We have health for our bodies,
>   all our material needs met,
>   and are set free from the law of
>   sin and death.[18]

So, when we receive God's salvation in Jesus Christ, we
receive a full salvation for the whole man, and, as we continue
in this salvation, walking by faith, we walk in all the good NOW
of what He accomplished for us on the Cross.

All this is summed up in the statement of Jesus on the Cross,
"It is finished."[19] Our redemption was then completed.

Having, therefore, deliverance from *all* the power of the
enemy, we are set free by the Truth and we remain free as we
walk in the realm of the Spirit. "Where the Spirit of the Lord is,
there is liberty."[20]

So, to live in need is to live in the devil's lie.

> Paul refused to live in the negative -
>   "sorrowful, yet always rejoicing -
>   having nothing and yet possessing
>   all things."[21]

---

[15] 1 COR. 2:12   [16] ROM. 8:32   [17] COL. 2:10   [18] ROM. 8:2   [19] JOHN 19:30
[20] 2 COR. 3:17   [21] 2 COR. 6:10

He did not say that he was not sorrowful, but he did say he was ALWAYS REJOICING. Paul did not live in his sorrow.

God could only give us a COMPLETE and PERFECT salvation, which would keep the whole man one hundred per cent free all the time as he lives in the Spirit.

The natural man will always be in need because of knowledge through the five senses, but THE SPIRITUAL MAN WILL ALWAYS BE FREE through faith in God's Word.

We know that *God is always committed to His Word.* Jesus said that we should live by every word that proceeds out of the mouth of God,[22] therefore He is always committed to us when we believe His Word. "I am watching over My word to perform it."[23]

"To be spiritually minded is life and peace"[24] and to live in anything short of fulness is to live an underprivileged Christian life.

"Of His fulness have all we received."[25]

We have a legal right to this life in the Spirit because of the righteousness of Jesus Christ. "The Spirit is life because of righteousness."[26]

We also have a right to all the provision of God, because He has made us JOINT-HEIRS WITH CHRIST, and "my God shall supply all your need according to His riches in glory by Christ Jesus."[27] "Shall He not with Him also freely give us all things?"[28]

The only way we can glorify and magnify the work of the Cross is by living *NOW* in the good of what was accomplished. The Cross is the end of the old creation and the beginning of the new.

ALL THINGS HAVE BECOME NEW — ALL THINGS ARE YOURS[30]

---

[22] MATT. 4:4   [23] JER. 1:12 (AMP)   [24] ROM. 8:6   [25] JOHN 1:16
[26] ROM. 8:10   [27] PHIL. 4:19   [28] ROM. 8:32   [29] 2 COR. 5:17   [30] 1 COR. 3:21

8

FAITH IN ACTION

When Jesus sent His disciples out, He told them not to provide for themselves, or, as the Amplified Bible puts it - "do not take a provision bag or wallet for a collection-bag for your journey."[31] - for He sent them out to GIVE, not to get.

They were to GIVE what He had given them and they would get their needs met as they went, for the Lord says, "Give, and it shall be given unto you."[32]

Jesus asked them on their return, knowing that He had sent them out with nothing. "Lacked ye any thing?" and they said, "Nothing."[33]

What a wonderful provider He was. He sent them out with nothing and they lacked nothing.

They went out in faith and came back in God's supply.

The will of God never takes us to any place where
> the grace of God is not sufficient,
>> the power of God is not enabling,
>>> or the provision of God is not adequate.

ALL OUR NEEDS ARE MET BY BEING IN THE WILL OF GOD.

If the disciples found this to be so before the Cross, it must also be the will of God for us after the Cross.

Jesus never taught His disciples to anticipate failure; they received their example from Him who never failed in all that He did.

So Jesus did not anticipate failure when He sent out His seventy disciples, because -

> they were *sent out from Him*
>> with His authority
>>> and His power
>>>> and His success.

---

[31] MATT. 10:10   [32] LUKE 6:38   [33] LUKE 22:35

They returned in triumph reporting one hundred per cent success.

So let us expect the same results when *we* are sent.

"As my Father hath sent me, even so send I you."[34] We are sent into this world with His authority and by the power of the Holy Spirit, to continue His ministry of life to all who need it.

Many are not going out today because they are waiting to get BEFORE they will give.

Reason will not let them go, for they are waiting to see before they will believe.

How different faith is. Faith acts on God's Word, attempts the impossible and expects God to do it.

"Freely ye have received, freely give."[35] The Bible also says, "Give, and it shall be given unto you; good measure, pressed down, and shaken together, and running over."[36]

What have we to give? All that Christ had to give, for we are joint-heirs with Him -

GOOD NEWS for the sinner,
    HEALING for the sick,
        DELIVERANCE for the demon-possessed,
            and LIFE for the dead.

He has sent us out intending that we should have no confidence in what we have in the natural, or what we ARE in the natural.

Everything that we have to give comes from Him, but WE ONLY SEE THE EVIDENCE OF WHAT WE HAVE WHEN WE BEGIN TO GIVE.

When He sent His disciples out they were not perfect, they were not professionals and neither were they specialists. They were just ordinary people.

---

[34] JOHN 20:21   [35] MATT. 10:8   [36] LUKE 6:38

If they had waited until all their needs were met, and they were holy, perfect and adequate, they would never have moved.

This is very encouraging to us "For ye see your calling, brethren, how that not many wise men after the flesh, not many mighty, not many noble, are called."[37]

So, God did not call us because of what we are, or what we can do, but -

He called us because of who HE is,
and what HE can do.

The moment we proceed to do the will of God, we automatically step out of what we are into what He is.

Wherever His will takes us, His provision is sufficient.

The early church lived so much in the revelation of the Holy Spirit that there was not one amongst them that lacked.

Surely this is our status in the Spirit today according to the Word of God.

Then why do we lack? Because we are not reaching out in this faith which God has given us and taking hold of His promises.

Paul declared emphatically, "Have nothing, and yet possessing all things."[38]

When we HAVE nothing,
When we ARE nothing,
When we CAN DO nothing . . . .

this in itself does not in any way hinder God from being all that He is and doing what He wants.

God is hindered in what he can do through us when we refuse to move by faith out of the negative state into the positive of what we have, and what we are, and what we can do through Christ.

Faith allows us to take possession of what we need for our bodies, souls and spirits, and to rejoice in the anticipated supply

---

[37] 1 COR. 1:26   [38] 2 COR. 6:10

11

- for the Bible says, "Whosoever believeth on Him shall not be ashamed."[39]

So now it should be the normal thing for all Christians to have their needs met,

> to have their prayers answered,
>> and to have God work through them,

instead of treating every answered prayer

> and every need met
>> and every work of God through them

as if it were some favour God had bestowed on them because they had pleased Him in some special way.

FAITH IN GOD'S WORD

So, beloved, I want you to get out that faith which has been lying dormant, and use it to enter in and POSSESS YOUR POSSESSIONS.

Take the shield of faith NOW and get back into the fight. Believe that the past is underneath the blood, then it will no longer speak to you of failure because you are living in the present of what God says - "We are more than conquerors through him that loved us."[40]

One warning - do not jump into the future for your victory and success. FAITH is the answer, not hope. Hope puts everything into the future, faith brings everything into the present time.

> You now live in the Spirit in the present
>> not in hope in the future,
>>> BELIEVING GOD'S WORD,

also believing that you have all the faith that you need to do His will.[41]

---

[39] ROM. 9:33   [40] ROM. 8:37   [41] ROM. 12:3

You must have faith now in the fact that you have faith because God says so.

FAITH, basically, is CONFIDENCE IN GOD'S WORD.

Even when you put God's words on your lips as a confession of faith, they come back to you through your ears. As you believe what you hear, you are moved from faith to faith, for "faith cometh by hearing, and hearing by the Word of God."[42]

We believe it in our hearts when He speaks and so He is allowed to bring His Word to pass. Quite often our head gets into the way, our reason wants us to be reasonable - but in the Spirit "we have the mind of Christ."[43]

Christ is the head of the Body and He plans and thinks for us. When reason says everything is all wrong, faith says it is all right.

God does not expect us to understand everything that He says, but He does expect us to believe it, and by believing what God says to us the Spirit of God brings us understanding, for "He will guide you into all truth."[44]

In the early days of my ministry I was asked to take a Bible Study, I realised that there would be people present who knew much more about the Bible than I did, and I was frightened that they might ask me questions which I could not answer. So I reached out to the Lord concerning this and He said, "They will never ask you a question about the Bible to which I do not know the answer."

I then saw that I could receive answers directly from God, by faith, as I needed them. God still expected me to study the Bible but, He could reveal by His Spirit, the answers that I could not find with my intellect.

> "But God hath revealed them unto us by
> His Spirit: for the Spirit searcheth all
> things, yea, the deep things of God.

---

[42] ROM. 10:17   [43] 1 COR. 2:16   [44] JOHN 16:13

> For what man knoweth the things of a man,
> save the spirit of man which is in him?
> Even so the things of God knoweth no
> man, but the Spirit of God."[45]

FAITH IS THE VICTORY

Faith always has its ear open to God.

Faith, therefore, is a right attitude of the heart towards God.

Faith is not what we FEEL, but what we BELIEVE.

The moment we believe God's Word and stand on it, this puts God on our side, which means the devil is defeated.

Jesus said to Satan, "It is written"[46] and He was virtually saying to the devil, "THAT is as far as you can come against me", because what is written FOR us is AGAINST the devil.

It is stated in the Word of God, "Ye are strong, and the Word of God abideth in you, and ye HAVE overcome the wicked one."[47]

You have as much faith in God as you have PROVED God by His Word.

Many people have emotional feelings toward God, which may not be wrong in itself - but faith has as its foundation the settled Word of God.

"For ever, O Lord, they word is settled in heaven."[48]

Our feelings can be up and down, but FAITH IS ROOTED AND GROUNDED IN THE TRUTH OF GOD'S WORD.

How many times can we remember feeling as if we were not saved, and how wonderful it was to come back to the security of God's Word.

Let us not build on the uncertain ground of our feelings -

---

[45] 1 COR. 2:10,11   [46] MATT. 4:4   [47] 1 JOHN 2:14   [48] PS. 119:89

14

God's Word is the same as Himself, so . . . .

Faith in God's Word is faith in God.

I do not always feel what God says I have, but I always believe it.

Remember, God is not always committed to us, but -

HE IS ALWAYS COMMITTED TO HIS WORD.

and once we are standing on His Word, *then* God is committed to US.

We are living epistles. The Word is saying what God says we are - so should our lives.

The world does not always read its Bible, but it does read its Christians.

God has given us -
>   not just words to preach to the world,
>   but a life to reach the world.

The world is in need because it only has the natural to supply its need, but we have a wonderful God who is rich unto all that call upon Him.[49]

We are here to advertise this wonderful life in the Spirit by enjoying all its benefits.

This is the abundant life which Jesus came to give. By comparison the world will see -

>   what they are out of, by what we are in, and
>   what they have not got, by what we have.

Jesus Christ is living today the same life that He lived on earth nineteen hundred years ago -

>   above sin,
>   above sickness,
>   above circumstances,

>   the life that had the answer to every man's need,

---

49 ROM. 10:12

> the life that defeated the enemy,
> the life that raised the dead.

This is the life that is in YOU. So, we should find all our sufficiency in Christ. Paul said "For me to live is Christ."[50]

FAITH SUBMITS TO GOD

Many people go to Bible Schools and Seminars hoping that the knowledge they gain about God will put them in a position to help others know Him. Knowledge is important but it is not what we know but who we know which determines the results we get.

Paul prayed that he might know Him, for "the people that do know their God shall be strong, and do exploits."[51]

Jesus had knowledge of His own,[52] but He was dependent on His Father as to how and when He should use it.

> "I am able to do nothing from Myself -
> independently, of My own accord; but as
> I am taught by God and as I get His
> orders. (I decide as I am bidden to decide.
> As the voice comes to Me, so I give a
> decision). Even as I hear, I judge and
> My judgment is right (just, righteous),
> because I do not seek or consult My own
> will - I have no desire to do what is
> pleasing to Myself, My own aim, My own
> purpose - but only the will and pleasure
> of the Father Who sent Me."[53]

It is wonderful to read that Jesus said He could do nothing of Himself, and then did everything.

Out of His subjection came His dominion. You ought "to walk, even as He walked."[54]

---

[50] PHIL. 1:21   [51] DAN. 11:32   [52] IS. 53:11   [53] JOHN 5:30 (AMP)
[54] 1 JOHN 2:6

He said, "without me ye can do nothing",[55] which means that THROUGH HIM WE CAN DO ALL THINGS.

Christ is not in any need at this moment, therefore NEITHER ARE WE, for "as He is, so are we in this world."[56]

"For in Him dwelleth all the fulness of the Godhead bodily"[57] and "of His fulness have all we received."[58] We are complete in Him.[59]

We are His Body - bone of His bone - flesh of His flesh.[60] WE ARE PART OF HIM.

He is the Head   - we are the body,
He is the living Word   - so are we.

We are living epsitles, born again of incorruptible seed by the Word of God.

When this Word, then, becomes flesh in our experience, the world will see Christ manifested in His fulness in the Church and through the Church.

So may this word become flesh in our experience that we might represent Him as He is. When this happens we shall go beyond our salvation to our Saviour, to know Him and not about Him.

We shall go beyond the healing to the Healer,
     beyond the baptism in the Holy Spirit to the Baptiser,
       beyond the provision to the Provider.

Oh that we might go beyond what God has given us to the God that has given.

Not to stop at being thrilled at what the grace of God has done for us - but to reach the God of grace.

WALKING BY FAITH

I believe, then, as we walk by faith in the Spirit, we shall not

---

[55] JOHN 15:5   [56] 1 JOHN 4:17   [57] COL. 2:9   [58] JOHN 1:16   [59] COL. 2:10
[60] EPH. 5:30

be begging, asking, pleading or crying for deliverance all the time, but we shall be praising and worshipping Him in Spirit and in truth.

How God must long for a people who have come together to give instead of to get. A people who will worship and praise Him for what He is, for God seeketh such to "worship him in spirit and in truth."[61]

We get so occupied with what we need instead of what HE needs, but I believe that as we praise and worship the Lord, all these things shall be added unto us.[62]

How many times have we been unable to worship God because of the nagging problems and difficulties we have brought to the meeting with us. Yet the Bible says, "How is it then, brethren? when ye come together, everyone of you hath a psalm, hath a doctrine, hath a tongue, hath a revelation, hath an interpretation."[63]

In no way can we read that verse like this, "when ye come together, everyone of you hath a problem, hath a need, etc."

Oh that we might give to God what He has been waiting for down through the centuries -

A people that are called by His name -
   who will walk in the provision of their God
      and in the blessing of their God,
         praising and worshipping Him.

A people advertising His wonderful love, both in their lives and, through their lives, to others - for the best way to advertise Christianity is to enjoy it.

God wants us to live in the Spirit - to walk BELIEVING - not feeling, not seeing, nor responding to anything that is negative, but RESPONDING TO GOD'S WORD.

Then we, too, will say with Jesus, "It is written, Man shall not

---

[61] JOHN 4:24   [62] MATT. 6:33   [63] 1 COR. 14:26

live by bread alone," (or circumstances, etc.) "but by every word that proceedeth out of the mouth of God."[64]

We can say, like Paul, in any situation, "be of good cheer: for I believe God, that it shall be even as it was told me."[65] or as Jesus said, "Peace be still."[66]

This is God's intention - that we should be manifested as the SONS OF GOD - heirs, JOINT HEIRS WITH CHRIST.

Tell, me, what heir and joint heir with Christ would be living in a need, when God had met it?

It is not wrong to have a need - it is wrong to live in it with the knowledge that God can supply it through our faith.

Now, beloved, God intends YOU to live -
> in His presence,
>> in His power,
>>> in His provision.

All that grace has provided is yours by inheritance, and your faith can reach every shelf of God's wonderful storehouse.

AUTHOR AND FINISHER OF OUR FAITH

Believe now that there is treasure in this earthen vessel.

No matter what you think of the vessel, believe that the treasure is good and perfect. The treasure is Christ living in you, but it is only as you share this treasure with others that you will experience the joy of possessing it.

> Freely have you received - freely give.[67]

You now give to live, but your motive for giving is love.

For God so loved that He gave -
> you are also to give
>> not grudgingly or of necessity,[68]
>>> but because you love.

---

[64] MATT. 4:4   [65] ACTS 27:25   [66] MARK 4:39   [67] MATT. 10:8   [68] 2 COR. 9:7

Faith is the key to receiving from God. Love is the motive for giving what faith receives. Paul said "faith which worketh BY love."[69]

So now you can take your eyes off faith and all that faith allows you to possess and turn your eyes upon Jesus, the author and finisher of our faith.[70]

Walk now as a son of the King. Having been released from your prison by the truth, remember -

The truth that SET you free will KEEP you free as you walk in it by faith.

[69] GAL. 5:6   [70] HEB. 12:2

CHAPTER TWO

From Healing To Health

GOD'S PURPOSE FOR OUR BODIES

THIS chapter deals with some of the problems faced by Christians who do not understand healing and health.

We are made up of body, soul and spirit. In the natural realm we have five senses to tell us what we have or do not have, but in the spiritual realm we have only God's word to tell us what we have for our body, soul and spirit.

Therefore, in the spiritual realm we receive healing first by God's word, then our bodies experience what our faith has already received. Healing does not come to our bodies first, nor do we receive healing *with* our bodies first, because we are not our bodies - we only live in them.

In other words, if healing came to our bodies first, we would not have to believe because we would know through our senses - which is not faith.

> We have to *believe first* -
>> that we are healed,
> then our bodies *receive* -
>> the manifestation of what we believe.

We find the original status of the physical body outlined in the first three chapters of Genesis. Man was created in the image of God,[1] and was therefore perfect because God was his creator.

The body, because it was perfect, allowed man to enjoy through his five senses all the wonders and benefits of creation.

Man's body did not become exposed to sickness until after the Fall. We can therefore conclude that the body was never created to be sick or to become diseased, because there was no sickness in the world until the Fall.

Even today the body still fights against disease naturally, for it was never meant to be diseased.

Sickness came as a result of Adam's sin, for man fell body, soul and spirit from the position in which God had created him.

The Fall put man at the mercy of the devil.

God later made a covenant with man to protect him from the result of the Fall, and as long as man was obedient, God was obliged to keep His part of the covenant.

"If thou wilt diligently hearken to the voice of the
Lord thy God, and wilt do that which is right in his
sight, and wilt give ear to his commandments, and keep
all his statutes, I will put none of these diseases
upon thee, which I have brought upon the Egyptians:
for I am the Lord that healeth thee."[2]

The Psalmist reminds us of the benefits under this covenant -

"forget not all his benefits;
    who forgiveth *all* thine iniquities;
        who healeth *all* thy diseases."[3]

"He sent His word, and healed them and delivered them from their destructions."[4]

The word was life to all those that found it and health to all their flesh.[5]

All this was only a temporary measure, for God was looking

---

[1] GEN. 1:26   [2] EXOD. 15:26   [3] PS. 103:2,3   [4] PS. 107:20   [5] PROV. 4:22

forward to Calvary - His permanent answer to the Fall.

Calvary did not have to redeem man from the curse alone, but it also had to deliver him from all its consequences.

This perfect plan of salvation for the *whole* man came to fruition at Calvary, when Jesus said -

"It is finished."[6]

saying in fact that God's temporary provision had come to an end, and His permanent provision was then legalised by Jesus' death and resurrection.

BEFORE THE CROSS

"He sent His Word, and healed them."[7]
"And the Word was made flesh, and dwelt among us."[8]
"As many as touched Him were made whole."[9]

Jesus was the Living Word, commissioned by His Father, for after He was filled with the Holy Spirit, and began His public ministry He said -

"The Spirit of the Lord is upon me, because he hath anointed me to preach the gospel to the poor; he hath sent me to heal the brokenhearted, to preach deliverance to the captives, and recovering of the sight to the blind, to set at liberty them that are bruised."[10]

Jesus stated emphatically that He had come to do His Father's will,[11] and then spent two-thirds of His ministry healing the sick. In doing so He revealed that it was still God's will for man to be healed - but -

---

[6] JOHN 19:30   [7] PS. 107:20   [8] JOHN 1:14   [9] MARK 6:56   [10] LUKE 4:18
[11] JOHN 6:38

23

all that He could legally give *before* the Cross, was what the Old Testament covenant had provided.

This provision was made solely for Israel.

Jesus gave them only what they were already entitled to have if they were keeping the covenant.

We see this more clearly in the case of the woman of whom Jesus said - "ought not this woman, being a daughter of Abraham, whom Satan hath bound - be loosed?"[12] He then loosed her.

The woman of Canaan was not entitled to deliverance for her daughter, as is evident in the story -

> "Behold, a woman of Canaan came and cried unto him, saying, Have mercy on me, O Lord, thou Son of David; my daughter is greviously vexed with a devil.
>
> But he answered her not a word. And his disciples came and besought him, saying, Send her away; for she crieth after us.
>
> But he answered and said, I am not sent but unto the lost sheep of the house of Israel.
>
> Then came she and worshipped him, saying, Lord, help me.
>
> But he answered and said, It is not meet to take the children's bread, and to cast it to dogs.
>
> And she said, Truth, Lord: yet the dogs eat of the crumbs which fall from their master's table.
>
> Then Jesus answered and said unto her, O Woman, *great is thy faith:* be it unto thee even as thou wilt. And her daughter was made whole from that very hour."[13]

Even though she was not entitled to deliverance for her

---

[12] LUKE 13:16   [13] MATT. 15:22-28

daughter, Jesus had to give, because her faith reached out for the crumbs that fell from the table. But it was still the *children's bread.*

In the case of the daughter of Abraham, Jesus accused the devil of binding her. Peter also emphasised this point when he said that -

> "Jesus went about doing good, and healing all that were oppressed of the devil."[14]

It is a great incentive to be healed when we know who has made us sick, and that

Jesus was manifested to destroy the works of the devil.[15]

Not just to give us healing -
but to GIVE US HEALTH.

BEFORE THE CROSS — HEALING

AFTER THE CROSS   — THE HEALTH THAT HE
                        LIVED IN BEFORE CALVARY

AFTER THE CROSS

On the Cross - Jesus "took our infirmities, and bare our sicknesses."[16]

"BY WHOSE STRIPES *YE* WERE HEALED."[17]

This was prophesied in the Old Testament in Isaiah 53:4-5, and fulfilled in the New Testament in Matthew 8:17 and 1 Peter 2:24.

As far as God is concerned, the Cross has dealt legally with sickness and now He sees us complete in His Son.

Our health is *maintained by faith in God's Word* - what HE says concerning the state of our bodies, not what our bodies say by symptoms of any sickness.

---

[14] ACTS 10:38   [15] 1 JOHN 3:8   [16] MATT. 8:17   [17] 1 PETER 2:24

25

He took our sickness in HIS BODY
so that He might reveal *His Health* in OUR BODIES.

Just as we take His Word for the salvation of our souls we must *also* take His Word for the health of our bodies.

After The Cross, "The just shall live by faith"[18] - faith in the fact that sickness was dealt with at the Cross.

We live *now* in the good of what the Cross accomplished for us.

Consider the physical condition of the disciples while Jesus was with them -

they were never sick -
but they *healed the sick.*

How odd it would sound, too, if we had read that some disciples did not return from their mission because they had fallen sick while healing the sick. Or even more strange if Jesus had taken a week off to recover from some sickness. This never happened.

If the disciples were in perfect health while they carried out God's will *before* the Cross -

what is our condition *after* the Cross
when Jesus is not with us - but IN US,
and the Cross is behind us.

Many Christians have been forced out of their ministry because of sickness and yet they were called to minister the Lord Jesus Christ, who is the "same yesterday, and today, and forever."[19]

The gospel that we have been given to preach delivers the WHOLE MAN from *all* the consequences of the curse.

Those who preach the Gospel should advertise this fact, on the mission field or at home. Many dear saints, because they have no revelation for their physical bodies, are prevented from

---

[18] GAL. 3:11   [19] HEB. 13:8

doing the will of God and serving Him in the way that they should.

This is not the condition in which God sees us, because of the finished work of His Son -

He sees us *whole* from Calvary to Glory.

Whether we appropriate this or not - it does not alter the fact that it is a FULL SALVATION for the *whole man.*

If we look at the early Church, we see them *IN HEALTH,* ministering healing to the outsider, and in their midst there was not "any among them that lacked."[20]

This was because every member was subject to the Holy Spirit, and with the gifts of the Spirit in operation, the Church was edified and built up by the functioning of the Body of Christ.[21]

God's full plan was that no sickness or disease in any form should prevent the saint from doing His will.

So, we remain in the world
to advertise His health,
and to heal the sick.

for the Church should be living in His health and ministering healing to those outside.

HEALTH IS OUR INHERITANCE

We are living epistles,[22] representing today the health that Christ has made legally available to us by His death and resurrection.

We are advertising His Health by glorifying God in our bodies.[23]

The Word is health to all our flesh.[24] "That the life also of Jesus might be made manifest in our body."[25] "That the

---

[20] ACTS 4:34   [21] EPH. 4:16; 1. COR. 12; ROM. 12
[22] 2 COR. 3:3   [23] 1 COR. 6:20   [24] PROV. 4:22   [25] 2 COR. 4:10

27

resurrection life of Jesus also may be shown forth by and in our bodies."[26]

By this we understand why John prayed that - "thou mayest prosper and be in HEALTH, even as thy soul prospereth."[27]

When we were born again spiritually, we were born into His complete life which includes His health.

Now we live in His health - sickness is outside us.

The only gateway in is through our bodies, but we are not our bodies - we live in them.

Having a spiritual life as well as a physical life, we have a new source of information for our bodies.

There is an alternative to sickness -
to live by faith in what God says we are physically, and *not* by what our bodies tell us.

WE DO NOT NOW RECEIVE OUR HEALTH FROM OUR BODIES - IT COMES FROM THE LORD BY HIS WORD. We live by every word that proceeds out of His mouth.[28]

We now give our bodies His health by believing His Word,

for it is not our bodies that tell us we are in health -

we tell our bodies.

God is committed to producing in our bodies the health which we receive by faith in His Word.

To live in health, we do not deny the evidence of sickness when we are attacked in our bodies - we are not trying to overcome sickness with our minds.

We are not in health by the *absence* of sickness in our bodies, but we are in health by the *presence* of God's Word in our faith.

We are not dependent on our senses to tell us that we are

---

[26] 2 COR. 4:10 (AMP)   [27] 3 JOHN 2   [28] MATT. 4:4

living in health, but on our faith in God's Word.

One important point is that we have to walk close to the Lord in our relationship with Him and not to abuse our bodies, in order to live effectively in His health. It is not something we have to attain to with our bodies or our minds, for it is our legal inheritance in which we live by faith.

It is *not* a sin to be sick or to remain sick, *but* that does not alter the fact that we are legally entitled to His health even if we cannot appropriate it.

If Jesus Himself were here in His physical body, He could not offer us more than what He has accomplished for us on the Cross.

We are bought with a price[29] - so we are God's property - and He has a right to state the condition of *His property.*

Believe, therefore, that you are in HIS HEALTH and walk by faith in God's Word concerning your body - remembering you grow in what you believe you are in.

TAKE THE WORD OF GOD FOR YOUR HEALTH - just as much as you have taken it, and trust it, for your soul's salvation.

Jesus lived in health to be free in his physical body to minister to those who were sick -

> advertising health
> > first by living in it
> > > and secondly by giving it.

FOR THE SICK

Many people are not healed because they question the Word of the Lord.

God is one hundred per cent committed to His Word,

---

[29] 1 COR. 6:20

therefore, He sees it fulfilled before He speaks. Faith allows us to accept His Word without question, when confronted by sickness in our bodies.

You may be in need of healing as you read this book. How do you deal with this?

First, realise that you have faith, not by your feelings, but because God says so.

Now, where does the strength of this faith lie? Look to the Cross. Realise that it was there that Jesus took your infirmities and bare your sicknesses,[30] and *with His stripes you were healed.*[31]

Sickness has been dealt with legally for you, so you have a legal right to be healed. Whether you appropriate this healing or not, it is still to your credit - included in your salvation.

Now, see Jesus bearing your sickness in His own body upon the Cross, as you once saw Him bearing your sins upon the Cross, and RECEIVE HIS HEALING BY HIS WORD.

Do not go to your body for the evidence that you are healed, but take God's Word for the physical condition of your body, just as you took that Word for the condition of your soul.

As you believe that your *soul* is in His righteousness,
Believe that your *body* is in His Health.

Remember now that your body has nothing to tell you outside God's Word and God's provision, but *you* have something to tell your body -

YOU ARE HEALED BY HIS STRIPES.

Do not try to get rid of any symptoms but *confess His Word* as the condition of your body.

You are what God says you are physically - not what the symptoms say.

It is ludicrous to deny the evidence of the symptoms, or to say

---

[30] MATT. 8:17   [31] 1 PETER 2:24

that sickness does not exist - we are not saying that the negative does not exist, but we believe that -

FAITH GIVES SUBSTANCE AND EVIDENCE TO THE POSITIVE.[32]

If your faith is insufficient for an instant miracle, you can still receive your healing by faith.

First, reach out to God and receive the complete healing of your body by faith. When you have the complete results in your faith, from that moment your body will grow out of the condition which it is in -

whether sickness, disease or deformity -
into the results that your faith has received.

Remember, your body cannot grow out of something unless it has something to grow into.

Faith allows you to receive for your body what your body cannot receive for itself.

Remember that you are living by faith in what God says you are physically - not what your body says.

God's Word is the last word.

Suppose you have applied all this and you are still sick? Then do not try to get healed by trying to get rid of the evidence of your sickness.

Many Christians will only believe that they are healed when the evidence of their sickness is gone - which means they are not taking God's Word for their healing.

Forget your sickness altogether and begin to seek the Lord for Himself. This will bring you to a place in His presence where the Word which you have received by faith becomes a living reality - and your sickness cannot remain because the Lord is more of a reality to you than your sickness.

Sometimes we become too involved in fighting our

---

[32] HEB. 11:1

symptoms and get dragged even lower, and it is nearly impossible for us to have faith.

When you pray for yourself, or when you have been prayed for, get occupied with the Lord until what you have prayed for becomes your experience.

Now that you have received healing by God's Word - a Word that is made legal by what has been accomplished on the Cross for you -

you can step out on it
without any extra evidence for support

because God's Word is the last Word - and He is watching over His Word to perform it.[33]

When you are prayed for, do not fall into the trap of saying that you are "trusting God for your healing" - He *has* healed you.

He is not going to heal you.
HE HAS HEALED YOU -
by the Word, not by the evidence of the healing,

and when you take the Word, *you are healed the moment you pray and receive that Word.*

All healings are instantaneous by faith, because faith is the evidence of things not seen.

You can lose your healing if it is based only on the evidence of your body - but you can never lose it if it is based on the Word.

---

[33] JER. 1:12

CHAPTER THREE

God's Prosperity

THE opening chapters of Genesis reveal the steps which God took to ensure that the first man would never be in need.

We see that man was never created in need, for God was his *creator* and *supplier*. God planned so well in love that not one detail of man's need was overlooked.

When we think that Almighty God planted a garden and put there the man He had formed,[1] we begin to see the deliberate plan of God to provide for man out of the best of creation. There is no record that Adam ever desired anything outside the garden, which shows that it was the best that God provided - sufficient to meet all man's needs.

The tree of life being in the midst of the garden, i.e. the spiritual in the midst of the material, helps us to understand how important it was to God that the material needs of man. should be met equally with the spiritual.

> God left nothing to chance -
> He wanted to be personally involved in all
> man's provision.

We only read about man being in need *after* the Fall, when he was driven out of the garden which represented God's provision.

> Adam and Eve fell
>   through sin
>   into need.

---

[1] GEN. 2:8

33

Man did not *enter* the garden in need, but he left it that way.

Yet God could not see him go out naked - and here we see the tender touch of a loving God. For the Bible says,

> "Unto Adam also and to his wife did the Lord God make coats of skins, and clothed them."[2]

This revealed also that God still loved man and wanted to take care of him.

All down through the ages, we read of God's provision for man. Sometimes this provision was miraculous, revealing to man that he was never meant to be in need materially.

How thrilled we are to read about the patriarchs - Abraham,[3] Isaac,[4] and Jacob,[5] Elijah,[6] David,[7] and Samson,[8] and that classical example of God's provision of manna from heaven and water from the rock for Moses and the Children of Israel.

> "And I have led you forty years in the wilderness: your clothes are not waxen old upon you, and thy shoe is not waxen old upon thy foot.
> Ye have not eaten bread, neither have ye drunk wine or strong drink: that ye might know that I am the Lord your God."[9]

All this shows us that at no time was God unable to meet their needs, for

> "The things which are impossible with men are possible with God."[10]

If David could say under the *old* covenant,

"THE LORD IS MY SHEPHERD; I SHALL NOT WANT"[11]

how much more can we say under the *new* covenant,

"MY GOD SHALL SUPPLY *ALL* YOUR NEED ACCORDING TO HIS RICHES IN GLORY BY CHRIST JESUS."[12]

In the New Testament, Jesus re-assures us with these words

---

[2] GEN. 3:21   [3] GEN. 12:2   [4] GEN. 25:11   [5] GEN. 35:11   [6] 1 KINGS 17:6
[7] 1 SAM. 18:4   [8] JUDGES 15:19   [9] DEUT. 29:5-6   [10] LUKE 18:27   [11] PS. 23:1
[12] PHIL. 4:19

that God is still providing for us:-

> "Therefore take no thought, saying, What shall we
> eat? or, What shall we drink? or, Wherewithal
> shall we be clothed?
> (For after all these things do the Gentiles seek:)
> for your heavenly Father knoweth that ye have need
> of all these things.
> But seek ye first the kingdom of God, and his
> righteousness; and all these things shall be added
> unto you."[13]

God's kingdom is not a kingdom of needs. It is a kingdom where our needs are met, not automatically, but as we believe that they *are met* by what Christ has accomplished for us on the Cross.

Sin put man into need, but -

RIGHTEOUSNESS HAS PUT MAN INTO GOD'S SUPPLY

We read, "though he was rich, yet for your sakes he became poor, that ye through his poverty might be rich."[14]

Poverty is a result of the Fall - not a symbol of holiness.

God is meeting our needs - but how is He going to have living witnesses that He has supplied all our needs -

unless we live in the supply?

Is it conceivable that God, who created the first man without need, should desire any less for us, *His new creation*?

Just as Adam was created in God's supply,

so *we* are born again into God's provision.

I believe it is the will of God that *all* His children should live in the abundant supply that Jesus Christ has made available.[15]

By His death on the Cross and resurrection, Jesus put man in legal standing with God, so that God could meet all his needs -

---

[13] MATT. 6:31-33   [14] 2 COR. 8:9   [15] 2 COR. 8:9

not according to his *need,* but,

ACCORDING TO HIS RICHES IN GLORY BY CHRIST JESUS[16]

HOW TO LIVE BY FAITH

To LIVE BY FAITH is to LOOK TO GOD ALONE to meet all our needs - taking God's Word for our material provision and recognising that ALL WE HAVE BELONGS TO THE LORD. This must be a continuous attitude -

> if He owns all that we have,
> > then we must own all that He has,
> > > by faith.

So you do not go to the natural to see what you possess materially - for you are connected by faith to the continuous supply of God.

FAITH ALLOWS US TO DO THE WILL OF GOD WHEN WE HAVE NO VISIBLE EVIDENCE OF HIS PROVISION.

This is illustrated in the Old Testament. Just as Elijah was sent by God to the widow to connect up her oil supply to the Lord's, so Jesus came to connect up our wealth to His - the visible to the invisible.[17]

> We do not live by faith in the visible,
> > but we live by faith in the invisible -

believing that we are connected to God's supply.

The widow's oil did not increase in the jar; the increase became visible only as she poured it out. She always had to use her faith, and, each time she poured she had to believe that she was connected to heaven's supply.

We, also, must not think and move in the limitation of what we can see we have in the natural and visible, but we must

---

[16] PHIL. 4:19   [17] 1 KINGS 17:14-16

believe that our supply is continually connected up to heaven as we give or use what we possess.

Though our five senses cannot see the provision of God, faith gives us the substance and evidence of things not seen.[18]

The whole church should live by faith - not just a select few that have been called into what we term full-time ministry, for EVERYONE should be a full-time worker with the Lord, whatever their job may be.

You do not become a full-time worker with the Lord by leaving your job or selling your business.

The Bible tells us the just *shall* live by faith.[19] I believe this faith must be invested in what God tells us concerning our material standing.

If all that you have belongs to the Lord - and He has the sole use of everything - then you *are* living by faith.

Even if you are a millionaire you can live by faith, with your bank account full and with several cars and houses. If it all belongs to the Lord *and He has access to it,* then you are living by faith.

LIVING BY FAITH WITH A REGULAR INCOME

If your income is given to the Lord and He is allowed to use it as He wills - even to the extent of taking the whole amount and using it for somebody's immediate need - you must then believe that you are living in His supply and that He will provide for you.

> IF YOU ARE LIVING BY FAITH, IT MAKES NO DIFFERENCE WHETHER OR NOT YOU HAVE ANY VISIBLE EVIDENCE OF GOD'S SUPPLY.

---

[18] HEB. 11:1   [19] HEB. 10:38

37

But remember, you *must not* give money away without first hearing from the Lord.

GOD SHOULD BE CONSULTED
ABOUT *ALL* THE USE OF HIS MONEY

Should there be a lapse of time in God's speaking to you about giving, there is no need for you to feel guilty, for it is still His money and He might want it to reach a certain sum before He uses it, either for someone else or for you.

If, therefore, all the money that you receive from working or from other sources belongs to the Lord, then YOU ARE LIVING BY FAITH and you are immediately connected to His supply.

To live by faith means that even though you have an income from a secular job, you are able to live and to give beyond your income if necessary.

Many times we hear the expression, "I have to work for a living."

We do not have to work for a living if we live by faith. God *gives* us the living as we work with Him in our secular jobs.

Should there be no work available, through no fault of our own, then God must still provide a living - but He expects us to work, if work is available.

We work now to make money available to the Lord, which He can use as He wills.

Now you are working with and for the Lord, not just for yourself or the firm - whether you are in an office, a factory, a hospital or in any other occupation.

"And whatsoever ye do,
do it heartily, as to the Lord,
and not unto men."[20]

It will then be noticeable that you arrive on time, that you do

---

[20] COL. 3:23

38

not leave before time, and that, in between, you do not cheat the Lord of time. You will naturally do a better job than the unconverted,

for you have *God's* strength,

His wisdom and *His* knowledge

available to you, so that He might have a living testimony that you are working with Him.

Since you are working with the Lord, no job should ever be boring - and, remember, promotion comes from the Lord and you do not need any references with Him.

If Joseph had needed references to become Prime Minister of Egypt, the fact that he was an *ex-jailbird* and *slave* did not give him the references people would require. Joseph prospered in his circumstances, and that is the "reference" that God wants you to have, if He tells you to change your employment.

You should never lose your job because you are not giving satisfaction to your employers.

Some Christians jump from job to job, leaving behind a very bad testimony.

I am very glad to say that this is not so in every case, for some Christians have a wonderful testimony wherever they work.

Others expect employers, who are Christians, to give them special privileges. Your employers are *not* paying for *your ability to preach* to their employees, and they feel that you should not cheat them out of time to do this.

I believe, however, that God will always make a way if He wants to speak, through you, to somebody with whom you work.

I have heard so many testimonies of Christians finding themselves in impossible positions, and God has answered in wonderful ways - even to the extent of making machines work by the laying on of hands.

In *every* job
THERE IS AN OPPORTUNITY
TO PROVE GOD.

LIVING BY FAITH AS AN EMPLOYER

If you are an employer and you are living by faith, then all your profit belongs to the Lord - and you are connected up to *His* resources.

You must then recognise that the Lord is your senior partner and what you do not know about the business - He does.

The Lord must be consulted
in *all* matters
concerning *His* business.

You must have faith either that God will give you the right employees, or that He will put them right while they are employed by you.

You must not be influenced by outward appearances, or even by good and bad references, but *you must go by the witness of the Holy Spirit,* for your place of employment can now be used by the Lord to minister to those that are in need.

Should you desire to expand your business -
then your SENIOR PARTNER
has made *unlimited* capital available.

If you have to buy or sell, remember, your Senior Partner knows the right time to do both.

WHEN YOU RUN OUT OF *YOUR* FUNDS,
YOU RUN INTO *HIS*.

Now, you do not have to think of the limitations of your business ability or your financial status. If you are God's businessman, then what you do not know about your business -

God does.

An employer does not have to give up his business to serve the Lord. God can bring his business to a place where it can take care of itself, leaving him free to preach the gospel.

If he later has to leave his business to preach the gospel, then it will be because he is successful. If he cannot prove God in his business, how does he expect to prove Him outside it? When your business is prospering, then God may call you out - but the calling of God is not a way of escape from a failing business.

I am sorry to hear that some men have closed down their business in order to preach the gospel; and in many cases they are not doing any *more* than they did when they were in their business.

I feel that an employer gives a greater witness to the gospel when people can see behind him a successful business. Also, while *you* are preaching the gospel, God can use your business to support others as well.

Warning -

The Christian employer today must remember that he is not dealing only with other competitors, as is the natural man - he is dealing with wicked spirits in high places, who will try to prevent his business from prospering and God from using it to extend His kingdom.

This is one of the main reasons why so many Christian employers are on the verge of bankruptcy and are becoming pre-occupied with the business instead of with the Lord. "Ye cannot serve God and mammon."[21]

The devil's two-fold purpose is to make you spend your efforts fighting to make your business prosper, and thus take you away from fellowship with the Lord. You are there to take your business out of the devil's hands and put it into God's hands BY YOUR FAITH.

---

[21] LUKE 16:13

41

"This is the victory that overcometh the world,
even our faith."[22]

HOW TO SUPPORT ALL FAITH MINISTRIES

If you are called by the Lord as a minister,
then you *must* live by faith.

Also, there must be some evidence of your calling, for it is not being ordained in some denominational church that makes you a minister.

Ordination comes from heaven by the Holy Spirit, and the evidence that men (or women) are ministers, ordained of God, is that they have a ministry. Then their ministry will open a way for them.

Some ministers reading this will have a fellowship behind them, or be employed by a particular denomination, so they will have a regular income. This should not prevent them from living by faith.

Ministers must not be tempted to prime their congregations in giving - remembering that, as ministers, they are representing God's supply (not their need) to the people. The minister must teach the congretation how to give, and God will do the rest.

If we make it easy for the people by telling them what we need, it is *our* faith that suffers.

Remember -   YOU CAN NEVER MAKE IT TOO HARD FOR GOD, so give Him a chance to try your faith.

If all ministers had to trust God for their income, they would have a greater incentive to seek the Lord, and ensure that their ministry was moving the congregation and building them up to hear from God and support the minister financially.

---

[22] 1 JOHN 5:4

Then, fire in the pulpit and support from the congregation would be guaranteed. The fault does not always lie in the pulpit, but at least the responsibility of being right with God lies there first.

Many ministers today are prevented from doing the will of God, and from making progress in the work to which He has called them, because of lack of financial support. I believe two factors must be taken into consideration here -

> The faith of the individual and
>> the obedience of God's children.

If every minister
> LOOKED TO THE LORD
>> to receive from Him what he needed,

and every Christian
> LOOKED TO THE LORD
>> to see what He wanted him to give,
>> then

the minister would receive *from* the Lord
and the congregation would give *to* the Lord.

GIVING

When God called me to live by faith and to look to Him alone for my income, I had first to learn to give before I was able to teach others to do so.

"Give, and it shall be given unto you; good measure, pressed down, and shaken together, and running over, shall men give into your bosom. For with the same measure that ye mete withal it shall be measured to you again."[23]

"Remember this: he who sows sparingly and grudgingly will also reap sparingly and grudgingly, and he who sows

[23] LUKE 6:38

43

generously and that blessings may come to someone, will also reap generously and with blessings.

Let each one give as he had made up his own mind and purposed in his heart, not reluctantly or sorrowfully or under compulsion, for God loves (this is, He takes pleasure in, prizes above other things, and is unwilling to abandon or to do without) a cheerful (joyous prompt-to-do-it) giver - whose heart is in his giving."[24]

"Not that I seek or am eager for your gift, but I do seek and am eager for the fruit which increases to your credit - the harvest of blessing that is accumulating to your account."[25]

Since giving plays such an important part in the life of the believer, we should give to live and live to give. Nature shows us this in a beautiful way -

> The birds give their song,
> > the trees give their fruit,
> > > the flowers give their scent and beauty -

they all have something to give, but it is the manifestation of life that allows them to do so, and it is the manifestation of His life in us that allows us to give -

> the song of the Lord,
> > the fruit of the Lord,
> > > the beauty of the Lord.

As the Christ-life comes to the surface, we begin to give - motivated by love, for love will go on giving for ever.

We are told: "give, and it shall be given unto you."[26] I feel that so many of God's children miss the blessing of Holy Spirit-led giving - not realising that this is a ministry, as Paul mentions.[27]

I have to be at the receiving end of many people's giving, and so I have learned a great deal for myself about *my* giving, which I will share with you.

---

[24] 2 COR. 9:6-7 (AMP)   [25] PHIL. 4:17 (AMP)   [26] LUKE 6:38   [27] ROM. 12:8

When I visit some places, especially if I am very heavily committed financially, God will not always allow public offerings to be taken. The reasons for this are -

> First, that He wants to try my faith and
> second, that He wants to teach His children
> to give.

I remember how I was tempted when a very rich person asked me to tell her of my needs, and said that she would be delighted to help at any time.

I said to her, "I am sorry, but only the Lord knows my needs and, if at any time you want to be used to meet them, He will always tell you if He wants to use you. By faith, I am living in His anticipated supply."

We must not fall into the temptation of trying to find an easy way out or trying to lift the pressure off our faith.

Those who feel responsible and desire to give *must* seek the Lord to know what they should give.

In every case where I have trusted the Lord in this way, without priming my congregation or telling them what I needed, God has spoken to a few people and all the needs have been met through them.

Immediately we say we are going to receive an offering, so many people reach for their purse or wallet, without consulting God at all. This is wrong. We must ask the Lord if He wants us to give, and, if so, then what we should give.

This is one of the main reasons why God does not always want me to take offerings. Unless I bring His people to a place of faith where they can hear from the Lord what to give to Him, I can bring them into condemnation, because their giving is not of faith, and "whatsoever is not of faith is sin."[28]

> They are giving to the church or to the minister -
> they have not asked God what they should give,

---

[28] ROM. 14:23

45

and they are not giving to Him.

The result is that many of them do not receive back from the Lord.

Also, by this wrong giving, a minister can be taken out of the will of God, by being given too much or too little.

So, if you know you are going to a meeting, pray first, and go prepared to give what God tells you to the person who is ministering.

If He tells you to give nothing, you must not give anything, because God might be trying that person's faith, or he might be out of the will of the Lord, and God could be wanting to reveal this by the fact that He is not supporting him.

Another reason could be that God is meeting his needs through the other members of the Body present - your money being reserved to meet another need, which the Lord will show you.

If you know a brother or sister is coming to visit you, either to minister or to be ministered to, open your heart to give and then you will never feel condemned afterwards as to whether you should or should not have given.

Even if you know a person to be in need, you must not minister to him unless directed by the Holy Spirit - otherwise that person's faith might suffer.

Also, if a person has come to your house looking to *you* to give, God can put this right by your not giving.

GIVING IS ONE OF THE MOST EXCITING MINISTRIES A PERSON CAN HAVE.

I could give so many testimonies of how God has told me what to give. He keeps my income balanced by what He gives to me and what He takes from me.

When all your money belongs to the Lord, how easy it is to

give - for anybody can give away someone else's money!

If you are entering into this ministry of giving, be sure not to consider what you will have left after you have given. Sometimes giving will test your faith - Jesus will say to you, "Do you love Me? Then feed My sheep."[29]

Remember your giving is an acknowledgment - just like the widow with her oil - that you are connected to God's supply and that there is no limit to what He can tell you to give.

If all God's children gave as God directed them - materially and spiritually - the Church would be transformed and, just like the early Church, there wouid not be one amongst us that lacked.[30]

As the Church matures we shall never even have to think about what we need, for it will be anticipated by Spirit-led giving.

> When we give our *money*
> we give *ourselves* as well.

> It is not *what* we give that matters,
> but *why* we give.

When you are really living in the Spirit, the natural offers you no security - and giving only puts you in a more secure position.

Some people have money in the bank as a security against a rainy day. This is only a support for their unbelief, and, sure enough, they get a rainy day. In many cases, the money lying in the bank is not serving any purpose, whereas, if God had been consulted about it, it could have been invested in His kingdom.

The Bible says that he that withholdeth tendeth to poverty.[31]

Many people, who are now walking in the Spirit, ask if they should tithe.

Tithing was Old Testament teaching for those who were under the law. The Holy Spirit could not lead them in what to

---

[29] JOHN 21:17   [30] ACTS 4:34   [31] PROV. 11:24

give, and so a set amount had to be laid aside - a tenth, which was called a tithe. Anything given beside that was called an offering.

Tithing is not taught under the new covenant. It was in operation up to the Cross, but not *after* the Cross.

> *All* our money now belongs to the Lord
>   and it is solely for His use -
>   as He wills and when He wills.

This means that your giving will go well beyond tithes, because you are giving *all*.

It does not mean, however, that you have to give all your money *away* to give all to the Lord. What He is not using for other people, He will be using for you.

You may be under the Old Testament revelation while you are reading this book, and you may ask, "Will God bless me if I continue to tithe?" Yes, He will - and I believe you should continue to tithe until the Lord really does have all that you own.

I say this because if some people did not tithe, they would not give at all. So remember that you are excused from tithing only if you are giving *all* as you are led by the Spirit.

> *How do I give* now that it all belongs to the Lord?
>   First, I ask the Lord if He wants me to give,
>   then I ask how much,
>   and, finally, I give that amount *to the Lord.*

There is nothing wrong with giving a regular sum to any church, missionary organisation, etc., but not without first asking the Lord.

Many times, a visiting speaker believes the Lord for his needs, but the congregation are not made aware of their responsibility in seeking God to give as the Holy Spirit leads.

Also, the people who are being blessed by the ministry of the visiting speaker must not be deceived into thinking that they are giving to him, if, afterwards, he is just given a pre-determined sum from the church. If you are supporting your church financially, you are entitled to know how the money is used.

Because giving which is led by the Holy Spirit is such an important ministry, we must be careful that our money is not tied up in pledges and other long-term commitments outside His will. Pray first, and He will reveal to you whether or not He wants His money committed to anything or anybody over a period of time.

Even if you feel you cannot support your church's work financially, I feel it is right before the Lord to give something for the heating, electricity, upkeep, etc. - as you would be expected to do in any other public building.

Many people have encountered great financial difficulties because they do not know how to give. Some have pledged money while convicted for their lack of giving, or while under pressure to give, or even because they were promised that God would give back to them much more than they had given.

They then get more distressed as they become more deeply involved in trying to meet a financial obligation into which, if they could have heard the voice of God, they would never have entered.

I am not implying that pledges or offerings are wrong, but our giving to them *can* be wrong, and, in all wrong giving, somebody suffers.

So let us listen to the Lord,
and not to man, or our feelings,
then EVERYONE WILL BE BLESSED.

"Inasmuch as ye have done it unto one of the least of these my brethren, ye have done it unto me."[32]

---

[32] MATT. 25:40

49

GIVING IS THE GATEWAY INTO RECEIVING.

"What things soever ye desire, when ye pray, believe that ye receive them, and ye shall have them."[33]

The Bible continually encourages us to ask and we *shall* receive. With the knowledge that you are blessing somebody else as you receive, you must always be willing to receive.

It has hurt me sometimes to receive from some people, especially those who, I know, have so little.

Yet the Lord says that I must receive, otherwise He cannot give to those who should be giving to me - just as Elijah had to receive the oil and the meal, so that God could supply the widow's need.

One of the great failures of the church today lies in not receiving.

Begging is not the way to receive.

"*Ask,* and it shall be given you,"[34]
       but do not ask the people,
         ask the Lord.

Very often we pray that God will meet our need, and we forget to receive the answer.

      God cannot give us what we ask for
         unless we receive it by faith
            before we receive the evidence.

We must be led by the Spirit in receiving from other people to meet our needs. Very often we ask God for the best, and somebody comes along and gives us second best, and we make do with it. Whereas, if we had witnessed in our spirit that we had received the best, we should not settle for second best.

I remember a person gave me a large sum of money one day, and then the Lord told me to return it. I held out for twenty-four hours, hoping the Lord would change His mind, but He

---

[33] MARK 11:24   [34] LUKE 11:9

did not. He then revealed to me that it would be wrong for me to accept this money, for the person was living in sin and God would not take anything from him.

I have experienced this again since. God has told me to return money that people have given, because it has not been given in faith.

We must be led in our receiving,
as well as in our giving.

Many Christians will sacrifice and pinch and scrape to give to God, and the Lord loves them for their sacrifice, but I believe He desires them to receive back from Him so that, when they give, their faith will be invested, not only into receiving their own provision, but receiving more to give.

If you expect to receive the best *from God,*
then HE WILL GIVE YOU HIS BEST,
but *you* settle for second best.

When I had my first large car, people would tell me that I could sell it and buy a smaller car and give the profit to the mission field. We cannot live in another person's revelation or way of thinking, and the mission field can only be helped by Holy Spirit-led giving - not just money.

There is nothing more wonderful than to begin to receive all that God has given - body, soul and spirit - and to feel free as you enjoy all that this life is continually giving to you -

knowing that IT ALL COMES FROM GOD
and He knows best.

PROSPERITY

"Beloved, I wish above all things that thou mayest prosper and be in health, even as thy soul prospereth."[35]

PROSPERITY IS HAVING ALL YOUR NEEDS MET,
with sufficient over to minister
to the needs of others.

---

[35] 3 JOHN 2

51

Prosperity is one step above just having your needs met by faith. *You* benefit by having all your needs met, but, through prosperity, the Body of Christ benefits by the overflow.

Jesus came to give us life, and that more abundantly.[36] We must live in this abundant life, giving our overflow to others who are in need.

God wants us to live in His prosperity through what Christ has accomplished for us on the Cross, for "though he was rich, yet for your sakes he became poor, that ye through his poverty might be rich."[37]

If the devil's children can prosper, then we have more right to prosper than they. The difference is that they must seek prosperity, but we have it added to us as we seek first the Kingdom of God.[38] They will realise that we are not seeking what they are seeking, but we are getting it. In seeking the Kingdom of God first, we get the best of both worlds.

God wants the world to know that He is our Father and HE GIVES ABUNDANTLY TO HIS CHILDREN.

PROSPERITY IS THE WILL OF GOD

and it is not measured by how much you possess but by how much you give.

You are not prospering, or in prosperity, until you overflow to others.

I believe the only way to solve the problem of need in God's children is to teach prosperity. You can bring food, clothes and money to a poor country, but you will still leave them in continuous need of the same things. It is much more important to teach them -

> to live by faith,
> in the revelation of God's prosperity,
> and to expect to give, instead of to receive.

---

[36] JOHN 10:10   [37] 2 COR 8:9   [38] MATT. 6:33

IF YOU BELIEVE THAT YOU ARE IN GOD'S PROSPERITY,
YOU *ALWAYS* HAVE SOMETHING TO GIVE,

just as the widow with the oil had something to give; it was so little, yet God connected it up to His supply.

I believe it is possible for anyone to prosper in *any* situation because of this revelation.

I feel that God is not limited in any way in this revelation of prosperity, whether by the absence - or the presence - of abundance, but it is a greater testimony if you can live in prosperity under the worst possible conditions. God is then the only person who is put at a disadvantage and

"IS ANY THING TOO HARD FOR THE LORD?"[39]

The Lord can prepare a table in the presence of our enemies,[40] and He can furnish a table in the wilderness.[41]

At this point, I should like to testify how God brought me out of the realm of just having my needs met, into the realm of HIS BOUNTIFUL SUPPLY.

When my wife and I were called by the Lord to live by faith, with only Him to support us, I hardly knew where to begin. For a number of years we would not take up any public offerings at our meetings, because I felt that by doing this, I was losing my status of faith. This was not right.

If we do not allow the people to give, we are robbing them, for the Lord says, "GIVE, AND IT SHALL BE GIVEN UNTO YOU."[42]

We wanted to teach everybody how to give, so we taught the people first to ask the Lord what to give, and then to give it as unto the Lord.

Therefore, we did not receive from the people,
but received from the Lord,
for only God could know what we needed.

---

[39] GEN. 18:14   [40] PS. 23:5   [41] PS. 78:19   [42] LUKE 6:38

Still most of my thinking and praying was taken up with needs. We never seemed to be on top of them, they always seemed to be on top of us, and when Christians came to visit us or we visited them, I was always waiting to receive something from them. Many times I did not minister to people's needs because I was in need myself.

I remember the day we had no money. We had no food at all, as we had finished the last of it that morning for breakfast.

We still had to set the table for lunch. Even though we had no food, we still had to act as if we had. When one o'clock came, which was our usual lunch hour, we sat down.

As we sat down, there was a knock at the door and there stood a lady with two big steaming plates of food.

She said to us, "As I was cooking this morning, something said to me, "Maybe Mr. and Mrs. Greenwood would like some of this." So I have brought it to you - I hope you have not started your lunch yet".

We said, "No", and thanked her very much and then we thanked God for his provision. Some money came in at the end of that day and we were all right again.

When everything was going well, we told the lady that God had used her to supply our need that day, and she was greatly encouraged.

I could tell you thousands of stories where someone has come up to me and given me just the right amount to buy my ticket home or pay for the groceries.

God has even allowed me to find money in the gravel on the way to the bus. Only God could have known that we did not have enough for our fare; and what we found made up the difference.

Finding myself in a certain city without any money for lunch, I said to the Lord, "It looks like a compulsory fast!" I was walking past a restaurant and the odour was setting my gastronomical juices aflame. I reached out to the Lord in my need, and He said, "Have lunch on Me". I never think when God speaks, because my reason would allow me to enter into fear of the consequences of my acting upon what He says.

I took a table as far away from the cashier as possible and with my back to him. I thought I would enjoy my meal much more if I was not reminded that I had to face him at the end of it.

As I looked at the menu, I thought, "Well, since God is paying for this, I will have the best", so steak was my choice. For one split second a thought entered my mind, "If anything goes wrong here, at least I am not washing dishes for a hamburger!"

As I sat there, I thought, "I am no different from anyone else in this restaurant with money in his pocket to pay for his meal, until I face the cashier with my bill." When the waitress gave me the bill, I went to the cashier's desk and found that there had been a change while I was having lunch. A different person was there, who recognised me as I recognised him. He was a Christian who knew me well.

He said, "Hello, Harry. While you were sitting down there having your meal, the Lord spoke to me and told me that I was to pay for it".

I wanted to test whether it was the Lord, or just my friend's generous nature, so I said, "I cannot accept charity".

"Honestly, Harry", he replied, "God really spoke to me and told me to pay for your meal". I then thanked him for being in the will of God and got out of that restaurant as soon as I could.

Later on, with a little more evidence of my prosperity in my pocket, I told him how close it had been, and he just praised the Lord that he had listened to Him and been obedient.

His only comment was, "You have got a nerve", but I knew I

had a God who would supply all my needs - even if He were forced to do so through restaurants provided for the public but run for the Sons of God!

If you have never received from God, you have no idea what it feels like to be on the other end of Holy Spirit-led giving.

My greatest desire was to be free from need. In desperation, I asked the Lord to show me a place where I could live *above* my needs IN HIS SUPPLY.

One day, I was talking to a brother and he said to me, "Do you believe that you are dead, Harry?" I said, "Yes". "For ye are dead, and your life is hid with Christ in God."[43]

"Then do you believe that Christ lives in you?" I again said, "Yes".

> "I am crucified with Christ, nevertheless I live;
> yet not I, but Christ liveth in me, and the life
> which I now live in the flesh I live by the faith
> of the Son of God, who loved me, and gave himself
> for me."[44]

He then said, "Well, is Christ living in need?" -

> "as he is, so are we in this world".[45]

Then the light came in and I rejoiced in my spirit. I stood up and testified that wherever I went I did not have any need. God had met all my need in Jesus Christ and I was living by faith in His supply. Prosperity had arrived at my door and I welcomed it in.

At that time a large cheque arrived to support my testimony of prosperity.

My deep desire for prosperity came out of the need to be free in the material realm, so that I could minister to those who were bound by it.

> To prosper means not to live in need, but
> TO LIVE IN GOD'S ABUNDANT SUPPLY.

---

[43] COL. 3:3   [44] GAL. 2:20   [45] 1 JOHN 4:17

When I started testifying that God had met all my needs, many Christians stopped meeting them. After a while, the money that I had in the bank was all gone-so was my testimony!

I was not saying so loudly or so often that God had met all my needs, for I had a pile of bills at home that were speaking to me more loudly than the revelation I had received.

The day before my first bill had to be met, I went across to the church and told the Lord the situation. I always make sure that I have my facts right, because, if I have believed something, I do not want to let go of it by my confession or circumstances.

I said to the Lord, "Is it right for me to testify that you have met all my needs while I have this large pile of bills, for I do not mind making a fool of myself, but I must not make a fool of You. Should I now go back to the old realm, own all these needs, pray and ask You to meet them, and then believe that You have met them?"

God said to me, "Pick up that Bible on the window ledge". I did so, for when God is speaking from heaven I obey immediately. He said, "Open it in the centre and read the first verse you see."

My eyes fell on this verse - "And in my prosperity I said, I shall never be moved."[46]

God showed me that I was moved by the bills and, if I only testified as long as I had the money in the bank, then my testimony was not in faith.

I put it right before the Lord, and I said, "Can I still own this revelation?"

He replied, "It is yours, if you believe that you have got it right now, in the face of all these bills".

I said, "Thank you, Lord", and I ran out of the church praising the Lord. I went over to my wife and said, "God has met all our needs, Hallelujah".

---

[46] PS. 30:6

There was no immediate evidence to support His Word, but we knew that we receive by His Word first, not by the circumstances being right. From that day - in 1964 - to this, I have been living in His abundant supply.

Oh, how I love Him for all His thoughtfulness. When I think He has only the Body of Christ to reveal his provision to me, it makes me want to be in a place where I can be used by Him to minister back to them, to show by what I give, how much He loves them.

As a Holy Spirit filled Christian, you *owe* it to the Lord to live in His prosperity, that others might benefit by the overflow from your life.

I am believing now, that this little book has offered you a key to your prison of need, and that you will walk out into God's prosperity, knowing that the truth which made you free will keep you free, as you walk in it by faith.

You do not measure your prosperity by how much you have in the material realm, but by what you give. Prosperity is having all your needs met with enough over to minister to the needs of others. If we are not thinking above our own personal needs, we are not in prosperity.

Never has the Lord anticipated that material need would stop any member of His Church from doing His will.

When Jesus sent the disciples out, He told them not to provide for themselves,[47] but as they went in the will of God, *the provision would appear when the need appeared.* When they returned, He asked them if they lacked anything, and they said, "Nothing".[48]

> They went out with nothing
> and they lacked nothing.

It is not what the natural tells you, but what the Word of God tells you that counts.

---

[47] LUKE 9:3   [48] LUKE 22:35

God does not want us to trust in what we possess
but HE WANTS US TO TRUST IN HIM.

Even after many years of trusting God to meet all your needs,
He wants you to continue to trust Him, for you will never reach
a position where you will receive anything automatically from
God.

You will always have to use your faith.

In prosperity, you do not ask God to meet your needs, for
your needs are met when you believe it, and moving out on this
fact allows God to bring it to pass.

Now you *think* what your need is -
then you *thank* Him that He has met it.

There is no necessity to pray for what God says you have
already by His Word.

For example, my children do not ask me for things to which
they are already entitled by virtue of the fact that I am their
father.

They do not say, "Can I have breakfast this morning,
Daddy?" And, when they go to school, they do not tell their
teacher that Daddy gave them breakfast that morning.

I have heard many Christians stand up and testify that God
has answered their prayer by supplying their need - as if it were
something new that God had decided to do.

God wants to free you from your need -
LIVING IN HIS PROSPERITY
BY FAITH IN HIS WORD -
praying for others who are in need.

People talk about George Muller's wonderful faith and all
that it accomplished. It was not just his faith, but he had a
wonderful God, who "is rich unto all that call upon him."[49]

George Muller is not here today -
but his God is.

---

[49] ROM. 10:12

59

"BELOVED, I WISH ABOVE ALL THINGS THAT THOU MAYEST PROSPER AND BE IN HEALTH, EVEN AS THY SOUL PROSPERETH."[50]

---

[50] 3 JOHN 2.

CHAPTER FOUR

Life in the Spirit

THE OLD AND NEW CREATION

THE Bible clearly shows that from the beginning, when God created man and woman, He created them for a spiritual as well as a natural relationship with Himself -

> a *natural* relationship with Him
>> through what He created in nature,
>>> and a *spiritual* relationship with Him
>>>> because God is a Spirit.[1]

God created man in His own image, therefore His creation was perfect. Adam did not *become* perfect - he did not have to grow into a relationship with God, or to progress spiritually. HE WAS CREATED PERFECT - body, soul and spirit.

We see a wonderful principle in the garden of Eden. God put the tree of life in the middle of the garden[2] so that all that was natural should serve the spiritual.

The spiritual was in the midst of the natural, so that Adam was never seeking anything outside the provision of God. God supplied adequately for all his needs - body, soul and spirit - in one place.

God created man so that He might enjoy his fellowship, and in return that man should be *completely* fulfilled.

When Adam sinned, he fell from the relationship in which he

---

[1] JOHN 4:24   [2] GEN. 2:9

had been created. He then found that sin had caused him to lose his standing with his Creator, for he lost the glory of the Lord and found himself naked, in need, hiding from God.[3]

Man is essentially a spiritual being. Though he may live a very sinful, worldly, materialistic life, he will never be satisfied until he finds God.

There is a part of him which is made to have fellowship with God, and it cannot be fulfilled by this world. It is a desire for a spiritual relationship with the LIVING GOD which cannot be gratified in any other direction.

We see the best in man, the deep longing and desires of the soul, expressed in music, art and other realms, but -

> man can never reach his highest until
> he comes into FELLOWSHIP WITH HIS GOD.

Whatever he makes for himself as a life will never be adequate and will never satisfy him until he finds the wonderful Saviour who loves him and gave Himself for him.[4]

God has done *His part* - reaching out to us through His Son, crucified on the Cross for us.[5] Now *we* must come to the Cross - to God's provision for our sin.

No matter what our need might be, the most important thing is our sin - and the Bible says that EVERYONE HAS SINNED. Every person is under the same condemnation for "*all* have sinned."[6]

> But God does not leave it there,
> for Jesus Christ came
> to deal with man's sin.[7]

On the Cross, He took man's place. His soul was made an offering for sin, that sin should be removed from every soul who truly repents and accepts His forgiveness by *faith.*[8]

Then *by faith* that soul is cleansed in the Blood of Jesus,[9] and

---

[3] GEN. 3:7-8   [4] GAL. 2:20   [5] ROM. 5:8   [6] ROM. 3:23   [7] MATT. 1:21
[8] ACTS 3:19   [9] REV. 1:5

by faith Christ comes in to that cleansed heart and lives His life in man and through man.[10]

The Bible says, "He died unto sin once."[11] There is no need for another sacrifice and there is nothing you can add to your salvation to make it any more legal or acceptable.

God's acceptance of His Son's sacrifice is all that we require to know for salvation, and is evident by the resurrection. It is not from man but from God.

THE CROSS IS WHERE THE NEW CREATION BEGINS.

You come as a sinner, maybe in sickness and poverty -
>   and there you leave it all on the Cross -
>   on Jesus, Who is *your* substitute.

Now believe that you have a right standing with God, because you are clothed with His righteousness and with all the provision that God has made for you in Christ.

"There is therefore now *no* condemnation to them which are in Christ Jesus."[12]

Man will always try to do something to attain to salvation or to justify himself in the eyes of God, but justification is by *faith* not by works.[13]

>   "For by grace are ye saved through *faith*;
>   and that not of yourselves: it is the gift of God:
>   Not of works, lest any man should boast."[14]

When we get to heaven, it will be purely on the merits of what Jesus Christ has accomplished for us on the Cross.

Many Christians cannot remember when they became a Christian. It is not always important to remember the date of your conversion.

>   You might not know *when* you became a Christian,
>   but at least you should *know where*.

There is only one place to start - and that is AT THE CROSS.

---

[10] EPH. 3:17   [11] ROM. 6:10   [12] ROM. 8:1   [13] ROM. 5:1   [14] EPH. 2:8-9

We shall not draw attention to the Cross or its effects until we start to live in the good of all that it has accomplished. Then the world will see Jesus Christ exalted and lifted up, and will acknowledge that His death brought life because *we* are living in that life.

He came that we might have life, and that we might have it more abundantly.[15]

Having arrived at the Cross, some people think they are at the end of the road; this is not so.

Many find it is not very long before they are back in sin again, and they are forever coming to the Cross - forever trying to get the victory over sin.

"Sin shall not have dominion over you,"[16] the Word of God tells us. Then what is the remedy? The Bible says -

> If any man be in Christ,
> > he is a *new* creation[17] -
> > > *not* a patched-up old creation.

"Whosoever is born of God sinneth not."[18] The new creation does not sin, but the old creation does. So we must put off the old and "put on the new man, which after God is created in righteousness and true holiness."[19] The new nature is not always seen because the old nature is still present with us.

Now let us take a journey to the end of the old man, and we are going to begin this journey at the Cross.

The old nature was crucified with Christ,[20] and *by faith* we must see this as a fact.

As Paul put it -

> "I am crucified with Christ:
> > nevertheless I live;
> > > yet not I,
> > > > but Christ liveth in me."[21]

---

[15] JOHN 10:10   [16] ROM. 6:14   [17] 2 COR. 5:17   [18] 1 JOHN 5:18   [19] EPH. 4:24
[20] ROM. 6:6   [21] GAL. 2:20

Again, if you are Christ's, you have "crucified the flesh with the affections and lusts."[22]

The old man, therefore, was crucified with Him, "that the body of sin might be destroyed, that henceforth we should not serve sin."[23] It is something that *has* taken place - something that has already been accomplished.

We *were* crucified with Christ on the Cross - and if you can see yourself there, that is wonderful. But it is only the beginning, for Christ did not remain on the Cross. He was also buried.

Now the old man *must* be buried with Him. This is a command for all believers.[24]

Baptism is God's provision for burying the old man - water representing the grave.

We do not bury people unless they are dead. "Know ye not, that so many of us as were baptized into Jesus Christ were baptized into his death."[25]

The full significance of water baptism has often been overlooked in the past; it is not just a doctrine but a revelation.

When believers are baptized by total immersion, they are not following Christ, but are being buried with Him - with a definite experience of being raised with Him to newness of life.

> "There is in every true baptism the virtue of Christ's rising from the dead."[26]

> "Therefore we are buried with him by baptism into death: that like as Christ was raised up from the dead by the glory of the Father, even so we also should walk in newness of life.
>
> For if we have been planted together in the likeness of his death, we shall be also in the likeness of his resurrection."[27]

[22] GAL. 5:24   [23] ROM. 6:6   [24] ACTS 2:38   [25] ROM. 6:3
[26] 1 PETER 3:21 (PHILLIPS)   [27] ROM. 6:4-5

65

"Now if we be dead with Christ, we believe that we shall also live with him."[28]

The old man is crucified with Christ, and then he is lowered into the grave and left there by faith.

Water baptism takes the place of circumcision. A part of the body is cut off in circumcision, and in baptism the old man is cut off by the operation of the Spirit of God.

The *old* creation stops in the grave
> because it has been sentenced to death,
>> and the *new* creation begins in its fulness
>>> on the other side of the grave,
>>> in newness of life,

because WE HAVE BEEN RAISED UP IN CHRIST.

> "In whom also ye are circumcised with the circumcision made without hands, in putting off the body of the sins of the flesh by the circumcision of Christ:
>
> Buried with him in baptism, wherein also ye are risen with him through the faith of the operation of God, who hath raised him from the dead."[29]

Now, free from the old man, "reckon ye also yourselves to be dead indeed unto sin, but alive unto God"[30] for "he that is dead is freed from sin."[31]

If we do not have faith in the operation of God, we shall go in dry and come out wet, but we shall not have a definite experience in which growth is continuous.

> By continuing in the experience of baptism,
>> we grow away from the clutches
>>> of the old nature.

We are commanded to be baptized in the Name of the Lord

---

[28] ROM. 6:8   [29] COL. 2:11-12   [30] ROM. 6:11   [31] ROM. 6:7

Jesus Christ.[32] In doing so we are drawing attention to the person who is responsible for what the act of water baptism represents, for we are separated unto the person in whose name we are baptized. That is why Paul asked the question, "were ye baptized in the name of Paul?"[33]

It is essential that we acknowledge the work of the Trinity in water baptism, for the Father raised up the Son by the eternal Spirit.

Because of the power which is in the Name of Jesus, very often evil spirits have been known to come out as people are being baptized, and also many sicknesses are healed.

The name represents the physical presence of the person, and we are commanded to DO ALL IN THE NAME OF THE LORD JESUS.[34]

Remember, now, that all which belongs to the old creation can only come as far as the grave, and "he that is dead is freed from sin."[35]

The Bible tells us, "ye are dead, and your life is hid with Christ in God."[36] This is a maintained state which we keep by faith as we walk in the Spirit.

Now that we are risen with Christ, the Bible teaches that we must "seek those things which are above."[37] "Set your affection on things above, not on things on the earth."[38]

Because of your free will, you must deliberately focus your attention on things that are spiritual, or above.

Your conversation is in heaven also. You talk a different language - a positive faith language - and every thought is in captivity to Christ.[39]

As you walk by faith now,
　　with your back to the grave,
　　　　and YOUR EYES FIXED FIRMLY ON JESUS,
　　　　this new life takes over *completely*.

---

[32] ACTS 2:38　　[33] 1 COR. 1:13　　[34] COL. 3:17　　[35] ROM. 6:7　　[36] COL. 3:3
[37] COL. 3:1　　[38] COL. 3:2　　[39] 2 COR. 10:5

"If any man be in Christ, he is a new creature."[40] This new creature is created after God unto holiness and righteousness.[41]

By this new creation, we see that God has not changed His attitude towards us. In His first creation, man was perfect. Is there any reason, therefore, to doubt the perfection of the last man?

As in the beginning man was created after the image of God,[42] so in the end he is created after God unto holiness and righteousness, to be conformed to the image of His son.[43]

So, through the death and righteousness of His Son, God has brought back man to right standing with Him.

We can assume then, that the right standing is for body, soul and spirit - but this time man has to appropriate it because he is already born into a natural world which has *not* made provision for him body, soul and spirit.

> Being born again of the Spirit,
>> man is brought into a spiritual realm
>>> where *all* his needs are met
>>>> as HE WALKS BY FAITH.

Because man was born into a world of need, his conversation and thinking have matured in this realm.

When he is born again of the Spirit,[44] he is born into a realm of God's supply, so his conversation much change.

> He must talk faith in the present tense,
>> living in the anticipated supply,
>>> while FAITH gives him the substance
>>>> and evidence.[45]

He is then free from the natural realm and its limitations to live by faith in the spiritual realm.

The new nature does not sin, for it is created after God in true holiness and righteousness.[46] "Whosoever is born of God doth

---

[40] 2 COR. 5:17   [41] EPH. 4:24   [42] GEN. 1:26-27   [43] ROM. 8:29   [44] JOHN 3:6
[45] HEB. 11:1   [46] EPH. 4:24

not commit sin; for his seed remaineth in him: and he cannot sin, because he is born of God."[47]

We conclude, therefore, that it is *impossible* for the *new* nature to sin. Some have become upset and felt that this could be termed 'sinless perfection', but many have been upset for the wrong reason.

They cannot believe that we can live above sin and that it shall have no dominion over us in this new creation. So there is always an excuse at hand for sinning, seeing that we shall always have this body of the flesh with us.

But the Bible says, "*putting off* the body of the sins of the flesh."[48]

It is still possible, though, for us to revert to the *old* nature and resurrect it. This is the reason why we must yield constantly to the Spirit, reckoning ourselves dead indeed unto sin. For the Bible says, "*if* any man sin,"[49] not *when*.

Sin is not something in which you must continue, but, *if* you sin, then provision has been made. Let me illustrate it like this –

If you asked me to build a ship that was unsinkable, I would get the most professional builders to do the job, scrutinising their work to see that the ship was perfect.

She would be launched when I was completely satisfied and then taken out on trial, proving that she was indeed unsinkable. You would then admit through logical conclusion that she was unsinkable, but there would still be a question in your mind – WHAT ARE THOSE LIFEBOATS FOR?

I would then explain that *if* anything out of the ordinary were to go wrong, then provision had been made.

If we sin, provision has been made. So let us rejoice now in God's provision.

If it is right for the new creature, as he comes before the Lord

---

at the end of the day, to believe that he has not sinned unless God reveals it to him.

He does not attempt the work of the Holy Spirit by trying to find sin, but he accepts that he has not sinned *unless* God reveals that he has. Instead, he gives glory to God who has kept him in this wonderful life where he lives and walks above sin.

Neither does the new creature spend all his time trying to attain to holiness. For Jesus Christ is "made unto us wisdom, and righteousness, and sanctification, and redemption."[50]

> "Put on the new man,
>> which after God is created
>>> in righteousness and true holiness."[51]

Our objective, then, should be to seek the Lord for *Himself* and *out of our relationship* with Him this new life will be manifested.

Some have tried to manufacture their own disciplined holiness - suppressing the old man and spending most of their time confessing and grovelling at the Cross - when they should be *rejoicing* as they are seated together in heavenly places in Christ Jesus.[52]

The new creature finds now that
> it is more normal for him to be victorious
>> than to be defeated -
>>> more normal to overcome
>>>> than to be overcome,

for he has been made to live in heavenly places in Christ Jesus, resting in His victory - not going out *for* victory, but going out *in* victory.

The *old* nature now being buried,
> comes to the end at the grave,
>> and allows the *new* creation
>>> to come to FULL MANIFESTATION.

---

[50] 1 COR. 1:30   [51] EPH. 4:24   [52] EPH. 2:6

For "if any man be in Christ, he is a new creature: old things are passed away" and "all things are become new."[53]

If the new creature is to represent Christ, then he must represent Him in *all* His provision.

Has God made adequate provision for the new creation? If He could make it for Adam, then why cannot we believe that He has made it for us? Paul, who proved God for himself, said,

"*MY GOD* SHALL SUPPLY *ALL* YOUR NEED."[54]

Then it is right to assume that if man lives in the Spirit, *all his needs have been supplied,* as he walks by faith in the supply.

It is wrong to say at any time that God has not made adequate provision in the Spirit - otherwise the spiritual realm would be lacking and there would be no advantage in being born again into *God's* Kingdom.

God can only fulfil His Word when we act on it. If He has promised, then He is committed to what He has promised.

Let us read a few of the many verses in which God has committed Himself:-

> "He that spared not his own Son, but delivered him up for us all, how shall he not with him also freely give us all things?"[55]

> "Of his fulness have all we received."[56]

> "Who hath blessed us with all spiritual blessings in heavenly places."[57]

After baptism in water, the first promise that the new creature must appropriate is -

> "That the blessing of Abraham might come on the Gentiles through Jesus Christ; that we might receive the promise of the Spirit through faith."[58]

> "For the promise is unto you, and to your children, and to all that are afar off, even as many as the

---

[53] 2 COR. 5:17   [54] PHIL. 4:19   [55] ROM. 8:32   [56] JOHN 1:16   [57] EPH. 1:3
[58] GAL. 3:14

Lord our God shall call."[59]

Many of my readers may have arrived at this point and yet have not experienced or even heard of the baptism in the Holy Spirit. Realising their lack of power, they want to experience this promise.

First we must see our need of the baptism in the Holy Spirit, and then we shall be willing to invest our faith.

That this experience is necessary is clearly seen in the fact that our Lord Jesus Christ was Himself baptized in the Holy Spirit when John was baptizing Him in the Jordan.[60]

Jesus did nothing before He was baptized in the Holy Spirit towards the needs around Him, showing that the ability to meet these needs should follow the baptism in the Holy Spirit. Peter confirms this -

> "How God anointed Jesus of Nazareth with the
> Holy Spirit and with power: who went about doing
> good, and healing all that were oppressed of the
> devil; for God was with him."[61]

So Jesus fulfilled the promise given in Isaiah, by saying "the Spirit of the Lord is upon me,"[62] and then moving out in the power of the Spirit to fulfil the purpose for which the Spirit had come upon Him.

Later He told His disciples to tarry in Jerusalem until they were endued with power from on high.[63]

He said, "ye shall receive power after that the Holy Spirit is come upon you."[64] They went into action even as He had gone into action, for He had said -

> "He that believeth on me
> the works that I do shall he do also;
> and *greater* works than these shall he do."[65]

The new man, therefore, cannot minister outside the power

---

[59] ACTS 2:39   [60] MATT. 3:16   [61] ACTS 10:38   [62] ISA. 61:1 and LUKE 4:18
[63] LUKE 24:49   [64] ACTS 1:8   [65] JOHN 14:12

of the Holy Spirit, and this experience must be appropriated BY FAITH.

Before explaining the experience, it would be good to understand the terms used in connection with it.

The gift is from God.[66]

Jesus is the baptizer in the gift.[67]

The believer is filled with the Holy Spirit.

When these terms are used, we must connect them up with the person to whom they are referring, whether the Father, the Holy Spirit or Jesus, but the terms are not important - *the experience* is.

John used the term "baptized in the Holy Spirit."[68] So we have to turn to Acts chapter two to see what the baptism in the Holy Spirit implies, and we read -

"they were all filled with the Holy Spirit, and began to speak with other tongues, as the Spirit gave them utterance."[69]

Speaking in tongues is not the baptism in the Holy Spirit. Being filled with the Spirit is the baptism in the Holy Spirit, and, as a *result* of being filled, you speak with other tongues.

We shall take note at this point that they *all* spoke with other tongues.[70] Peter spoke of this experience - being baptized in the Spirit - as a fulfilment of Joel's prophecy, and referred to speaking in tongues as part of that prophecy, as his words clearly show.

"Therefore being by the right hand of God exalted, and having received of the Father the promise of the Holy Spirit, he hath shed forth this, which ye now see *and hear*."[71]

If anyone were to come to me and say they had been baptized in the Holy Spirit but had not spoken in tongues, I would not question their experience of the baptism, but I would believe

---

[66] ACTS 2:39 and ACTS 11:17   [67] MATT. 3:11   [68] MATT. 3:11 and LUKE 3:16
[69] ACTS 2:4   [70] ACTS 2:4   [71] ACTS 2:33

73

that sooner or later they would begin to speak with other tongues - but *not* because they have to prove by speaking in tongues that they are baptized in the Spirit.

I feel that the spiritual benefit which follows speaking in tongues is essential for a person's personal progress in the baptism in the Holy Spirit.

The reason for being filled with the Holy Spirit is not just that we might live a full Christian life, but that we should receive POWER to minister that life.

This is not an experience of sanctification, though it can bring you closer to the Lord and make what you possess a greater reality.

Sanctification begins in the nature of the new creature, and should come into fulness after water baptism when we put off the old man and walk in newness of life.

> "And that ye put on the new man,
>   which after God is created
>   in righteousness and true holiness."[72]

> Jesus was endued with power
>   not to *live* a good life
>   but to *minister* that life.

Because there is so much emphasis laid on the glossalalia, let us now deal with this manifestation and put it into its context.

Speaking in tongues is under the will of the individual when he is outside the church, and under the will of the Holy Spirit in a church meeting. When you are in your own private devotions, you can speak at will. Paul said, "I will pray with the spirit, and I will pray with the understanding also."[73]

The will to speak lies with *you,* not with the Holy Spirit, for speaking in tongues is a vehicle to carry to God what you want to say in your spirit.

---

[72] EPH. 4:24   [73] 1 COR. 14:15

It is a means of expressing in the spirit
the things which are inexpressible
in natural language.

When we speak in tongues, unless we believe we are speaking to God, we are only doing vocal exercises. "For he that speaketh in an unknown tongue speaketh not unto men, but unto God."[74]

So many people are speaking in tongues and are trying to get something from God with their *feelings* -

instead of trying to get to God with their *FAITH.*

The more you speak in tongues, the more you will develop your spiritual sensitivity in the spirit beyond your mind.

Your mind tends to control you. It seeks to dominate everything that you are doing and wants to question it and analyse it - but this is not God's way.

Therefore, He has given us a manifestation which is beyond the reach of our minds, so that the mind might come under the subjection of the Spirit.

Because the Lord has given this gift of speaking in tongues, its use determines its importance. In Corinthians we see Paul stopping the abuse and directing the use of the gift. This, of course, was in the church - not in the private life of the individual.

The private life of the individual is revolutionized by this wonderful gift. A person praying in tongues can reach out and pray in the spirit, not knowing and not understanding the need of the person for whom he is praying, but feeling fully confident that the Spirit is praying through him.

The Christian who suffers from nerves before an event will find speaking in tongues invaluable.

The person who is involved intellectually finds rest and peace

---

[74] I COR. 14:2

and is renewed in the spirit of his mind[75] when he begins to speak in other tongues.

Having, therefore, your prayer life and your worship revolutionized, no wonder Paul said, "I would that ye all spake with tongues."[76] This also is my prayer for you.

> We must bear in mind
> > that the baptism in the Holy Spirit
> > > is a *gateway* into a continuous experience,
> > > and not a goal in itself.

When you go through this gateway, you enter into the supernatural - and as a result of this experience all nine gifts of the Holy Spirit are made available to you as *He* wills.

The gifts are manifestations of the Spirit, and they remain with the Holy Spirit. You are only the channel or the means whereby these gifts are expressed.

It will be good for your pride to remember that the Holy Spirit is the giver and still retains the gifts.

> So, you have access to all nine gifts.
> > You may not be used for all nine,
> > > but potentially they are all there
> > > IN THE HOLY SPIRIT.

Potentially, the whole fruit of the Spirit is also available; this fruit has to be brought out, as the gifts have to be brought out, to meet the occasion and the demand. But we must not *try to produce* either the fruit or the gifts.

> Paul said *desire* spiritual gifts[77] -
> > he did not tell us to ask for them,

You do not have to ask for what you already possess by God's Word.

> We do not possess what we *feel* we have,
> > but what we *believe* we have.

---

[75] EPH. 4:23   [76] 1 COR. 14:5   [77] 1 COR 14:1

We have to move out in the gifts, desiring to be used by God - not for ourselves but for the edifying of the Body.

After you are baptized in the Holy Spirit, you are not fighting against flesh and blood, but against spiritual wickedness or wicked spirits in high places.[78]

> Instead of being challenged constantly
> by the enemy,
> *you* are now in a position
> to challenge him,

and you will notice a greater conflict in every area of your life.

You will find yourself dealing with the devil directly in every situation, and overcoming in the power of the Holy Spirit.

Many of you may now desire this experience of baptism in the Holy Spirit because of the standing it gives you with God and the victory it gives you over the devil. Here is how you may come into it.

Jesus said, "If any man thirst, let him come unto me, and drink."[79] If you come thirsty, there will be no question in your mind.

Jesus then invites us to drink of the water freely, and BY FAITH we drink. Then He has promised that out of our innermost being shall flow rivers of living water.[80]

RECEIVE THE PROMISE BY FAITH, and now believe that you are filled with the Holy Spirit, and that as you release this power through your lips you will speak in another tongue.

Remember, the Holy Spirit has no lips or vocal chords or tongue of His own - He must use yours

> The sound is what *you* produce,
> but the language is what *He* produces.
> The sound is natural,
> the language is supernatural.

---

[78] EPH. 6:12   [79] JOHN 7:37   [80] JOHN 7:38

77

In the first experience, they, "began to speak"[81] - so must you, to give the means of expression to the Holy Spirit.

You must not listen to yourself or try to analyse your speaking in tongues, or you will quench the Spirit and you will not witness to your experience.

If you listen to yourself speaking in tongues, your mind will take over and repeat what you say, for the mind wants to get back into control. Remember, this experience is not to be analysed but to be believed.

If you speak our loudly and clearly, the Holy Spirit will take over completely. You will not be conscious of any effort under His control, but *do not* measure the depth of your experience by how well you can or cannot speak in tongues.

> As a result of this experience,
> the Lord Jesus will become
> a wonderful reality
> in *your* life.

You will find it much easier to communicate with Him, and you will become more sensitive to the leading and direction of the Holy Spirit. Your prayer life and your worship will be revolutionized.

It is important that, after being baptized in the Holy Spirit, you should desire to be used in ministry.

Many have dried up because they have not continued to speak in tongues and pour out in ministry. Only a vessel which is pouring out needs to continue to be filled.

YOU NOW LIVE IN WHAT YOU GIVE

This should be enough incentive for anyone who loves the Lord to be baptized in the Holy Spirit!

So, now *believe* that in this act the natural and the spiritual are united in GLORIFYING GOD.

---

[81] ACTS 2:4

To understand fully the life that Jesus came to give, we must see the position into which He has put us.

This life begins at *spiritual* birth. We are born of the Spirit, so it is our *nature* to be spiritual.[82]

The spiritual man has put off the old nature at baptism and has been filled with the Holy Spirit.

These are the bare essentials for him to begin to live and walk in the spirit, and *all* this is included in his FULL SALVATION.

The spiritual man lives in the Kingdom of God
because he was born into this spiritual realm.

There is only one mind in the spirit - THE MIND OF CHRIST[83] - which is a spiritual mind.

"To be spiritually minded is life and peace,"[84] so he must be continually renewed in the spirit of his mind, for the battle today lies in the realm of the mind.

Paul said, "be not conformed to this world: but be ye transformed by the renewing of your mind,"[85] bringing every thought into captivity to Christ.[86]

The spiritual mind is not limited to the intelligence or the intellectual ability to reason, so there are *no* limitations to the revelation which it can receive.

In the spirit, even an unlearned person can have revealed to his *spiritual* mind the most profound truth that no *natural* mind could comprehend.

The spiritual man has peace of mind because he knows that God has said He "hath not given us the spirit of fear; but of power, and of love, and of a sound mind."[87]

Living in the Spirit, the spiritual man is free from the limitations of his five senses, therefore it is imperative that HE LIVES BY FAITH in what God says and reveals.

He is completely dependent on the Lord

---

[82] JOHN 3:6   [83] 1 COR. 2:16   [84] ROM. 8:6   [85] ROM. 12:2   [86] 2 COR. 10:5
[87] 2 TIM. 1:7

for all His leadings and promptings.

He only moves as he is moved by the Spirit, for the Bible says,

"as many as are led by the Spirit of God,
they are the sons of God."[88]

So, with full assurance, he can step out of his boat of feelings on to the *solid foundation* of HIS WORD.

Every step in the Holy Spirit is planned by God - therefore each step is one step ahead of the devil.

Only when the spiritual man stops walking in the Spirit does the devil catch up with him.

"Faith which worketh by love"[89]
is the reason and motive
for living and walking in the spirit.

The foundation for love is trust - trust in the Shepherd who is going before.

So the spiritual man is making a way in the *invisible* or spiritual realm which will be *visible* to those who will follow - just as Jesus was the way by His life.

Jesus was a manifestation of the invisible God, revealing God's way in the visible realm.

The spiritual man has access to ALL POWER -
he has access to all provision
for his body, soul and spirit.

So he never goes out in need. He goes out by faith in the anticipated supply - believing that when he comes to the end of the visible he moves by faith into the invisible supply. FAITH gives him the substance and evidence.[90]

LIVING BY FAITH
IS NATURAL
TO THE SPIRITUAL MAN.

He lives by every word that proceeds out of the mouth of

---

[88] ROM. 8:14   [89] GAL. 5:6   [90] HEB. 11:1

God.[91] This is his natural food, the LIVING WORD - not the letter, but the Word that proceeds out of the mouth of God.

The spiritual man is not satisfied with what comes from the soulish realm, nor does he stop at praise.

He goes on to worship
IN SPIRIT AND IN TRUTH.[92]

What comes out of God's mouth must first be taken in by the spiritual man before it can come out to feed others.

God's Word becomes the spiritual man's weapon
in the spiritual warfare,
for it is the sword of the spirit.[93]

God's Word gives the spiritual man authority. Our authority comes out of the position that Christ is in now - His power and dominion and authority.

Individually we have authority over all that Christ has authority over, but we will never know or possess this authority until we submit to Him - then we have as much authority as we are submitted to.

Our authority is not over people - but over what is wrong in people and what comes against them.

Each individual has authority over everything that comes against - for he has authority over Satan in the name of Jesus - the name which represents all authority.

The Lord has set ministries in the Church and has given them authority over what comes against the Church.

He has set husbands in families to have authority over what comes against the families.

This authority does not come out of a position which has been given by man - but which is given by God.

All ministers set in the Body of Christ, especially pastors, have authority over everything that would come against the

---

[91] MATT. 4:4   [92] JOHN 4:24   [93] EPH. 6:17

sheep put in their care. If the sheep do not submit to the authority which is in the minister who has been made their shepherd, they do not come under the protection of that authority.

Similarly, if the family do not submit to the authority of the head of the house, they do not come under the protection of that authority.

If a pastor or leader is criticised by an individual or group, that ministry is quenched as far as the edification and protection of the individual or group is concerned.

Similarly, if any member of a family criticises the head, they cut themselves off from the edification and protection which God has made available to them.

We must believe that God has given these ministries and must draw them out by our faith and love.

If the minister or head of the house is not going on with God, then their congregation or family must find a place in love where they do not enter into criticism, but find a place which will draw the minister or head of the house back to their rightful place.

No ministers or heads of families should have to inflict the law of submission on their congregations or families, but should find a place in the love of God which will cause them to submit.

WE SHOULD NOT APPLY BY LAW WHAT WE SHOULD BE BRINGING ABOUT BY LOVE.

Submit one to the other in love.

Submission and sacrifice is a natural outcome of love.

The Word of God brings believers to a place of authority over everything that the enemy can bring against them, whether it be in body, soul or spirit, so that they can remain free, with authority over everything that would prevent them and others from walking in freedom.

The Word that is written for the spiritual man, is written against the enemy - so, by believing the Word, the enemy is dealt with.

Whether it be circumstances, sickness,
or the devil attacking you directly in any form,
GOD'S WORD HAS *ALREADY* OVERCOME —

therefore it will overcome for the spiritual man personally *as he uses it.*

The spiritual man does not live in his feelings -
his feelings tell him nothing,
unless they agree with the Word of God.

He is not up one day and down the next. When he attends a meeting he does not spend half the time trying to find God with his feelings.

God is no further than his believing away, and there is joy and peace in believing.[94]

Because the Bible tells the spiritual man his position and condition, he is at liberty to say what God says he is, and has, and can do IN CHRIST.

"That the communication of thy faith may become
effectual by the acknowledging of every good
thing which is in you in Christ Jesus."[95]

The spiritual man is more than a conqueror -
because God says he is.[96]

The spiritual man lives in health, by faith in God's Word which is health to all his flesh.[97] He is therefore free to minister healing to the sick.

He is also free to give, because he believes that God is supplying all his needs.

---

[94] ROM. 15:13   [95] PHILEMON 6   [96] ROM. 8:37   [97] PROV. 4:22

He has been born into God's kingdom, in all that God has supplied. It is his by inheritance, for "shall he not with him also freely give us all things."[98] "Of his fulness have all we received"[99] for He "hath blessed us with all spiritual blessings."[100]

Let us now see the standing of the spiritual man. He has access to the fruit of the spirit and to all nine gifts, made available in the Holy Spirit. He is therefore a natural able minister of this wonderful new life.

The spiritual man's sole purpose is to glorify Jesus Christ, and he is able to do this through the leading of the Holy Spirit.[101]

God has put *no limits* on the spiritual man.
HE CAN DO *ALL* THINGS THROUGH CHRIST
WHO STRENGTHENS HIM.[102]
He appropriates *all* that God has made available.

So, he does not live in the future in hope,
neither does he live in the past
in what God *has* done,

for there is only one time for the spiritual man and that is God's eternal NOW.

He does not work *for* God, but he works *with* God.

By living in the Spirit and walking there, he is right up to date in what God is doing *now*.

The spiritual man is connected to the full work of God in the *whole* Body of Christ, so that he is constantly contributing to that Body in life and word and deed.

The spiritual man's position in the whole Church (or Body) is that he is a LIVING STONE, built into God's house for an habitation of the Spirit.[103] He supports other stones as he also is supported.

The spiritual man is moved directly by God, so he can trust

---

[98] ROM 8:32   [99] JOHN 1:16   [100] EPH. 1:3   [101] JOHN 16:14   [102] PHIL. 4:13
[103] EPH 2:22

84

that -

> what he *feels* is God,
>> what he *does* is God -

and the witness of the Spirit confirms this.

There is only harmony in the Spirit, so he is committed to keeping this unity [104] until the Spirit, leading the whole Church into all truth, brings us into the unity of the faith.[105]

> God is preparing a WHOLE BODY,
>> living in the Spirit,
>>> to bring to birth a full revelation
>>> and manifestation of Christ.

The spiritual man's aim is to this end, and when Christ returns He will be coming for a Church that is living and walking in the Spirit[106] - in all that God says it is and has and can do.

> It will be seen by the world
>> that the Church is without spot
>> or blemish.[107]

All glory to the finished work of Calvary, the life of Jesus Christ, the Father's wonderful love, and the work of the Holy Spirit.

AMEN.

---

[104] EPH. 4:3   [105] EPH. 4:13   [106] GAL. 5:25   [107] EPH. 5:27

After reading this book those who are interested in its future ministry, and wish to finance its publication in other countries where they cannot afford to buy it, feel free as the Holy Spirit leads to send your cheques to Torbay Publishing, also stipulate the country you desire the book to be printed in. Please supply your name and address and whenever the book is published in that country you will be sent a copy free.

TORBAY PUBLISHING,
31 UPPER HEADLAND PARK ROAD,
PAIGNTON, DEVON.